DATE DUE

Seeing
Is Believing

Seeing Is Believing

How the New Art of Visual
Management Can Boost Performance
Throughout Your Organization

Stewart Liff and
Pamela A. Posey

AMACOM

American Management Association

New York • Atlanta • Brussels • Chicago • Mexico City • San Francisco
Shanghai • Tokyo • Toronto • Washington, D.C.

This publication is designed to provide accurate and authoritative
information in regard to the subject matter covered. It is sold with
the understanding that the publisher is not engaged in rendering
legal, accounting, or other professional service. If legal advice or
other expert assistance is required, the services of a competent
professional person should be sought.

Library of Congress Cataloging-in-Publication Data

Liff, Stewart.
     Seeing is believing : how the new art of visual management can boost
performance throughout your organization / Stewart Liff and Pamela A. Posey.
          p.   cm.
     Includes index.
     ISBN 0-8144-0808-7
     1. Communication in management—Audio-visual aids.   2. Communication
in organizations—Audio-visual aids.   3. Visual communication.   4. Employee
motivation.   I. Posey, Pamela Ashley.   II. Title.

HD30.3.L53   2004
658.4' 5—dc22

                                                                    2004012592

Printing number

10   9   8   7   6   5   4   3   2   1

CONTENTS

ACKNOWLEDGMENTS

Books are rarely the sole work of those whose names appear on the cover. This one is no exception. So many people have influenced us over the years that it is impossible to personally thank each and every one of them here. Yet, there are some whose contributions are so significant that we must single them out for special thanks.

First, we wish to acknowledge the exceptional support we received from Adrienne Hickey, our editor. Her unfailing encouragement, her direct manner, her wonderfully wry sense of humor, and her commitment to keep this project moving forward have made our first book project as much fun and as painless as writing a book can be. Adrienne, you are the best! We also owe thanks to Jim Bessent and Andy Ambraziejus from AMACOM for their critical insights and technical support. We especially appreciated Jim's clear focus on getting this book produced and his frequent references to being ahead of schedule!

We also wish to thank those companies and all of the people in them who shared their visual management experiences with us. Special thanks for serving as our primary points of contact go to Victor Gill of Burbank Airport; Lynn Maguire and Denise Glesing of Columbus Regional Hospital; Lida Dersookian of Leo A. Daly, Inc.; Dana Judge and Robin Bardell of Hewlett-Packard Financial Services; Dr. Gary Cohn, Superintendent of the Port Angeles School District in Port Angeles, Washington; Marjie Shahani of QTC; Dan Goetz of

UVDI; and Bruce Diamond of ZiLOG. In addition, Peter Durand of Alphachimp Studios; Gordon Rudow of Bonfire Communications; Ann Hermann-Nehdi of Hermann International; and James Haudan and Christy Stone of Root Learning, Inc of Maumee, Ohio, shared their own work in the visual learning arena with us, and graciously allowed us to use it in this book. To each and every one of you, we extend our gratitude and wish you continued success in this visual world.

We also have many colleagues who have given their time and energy to us in a variety of ways, and a few deserve special recognition. For Stew, the advice of mentors Tom Lastkowka, Bill Snyder, and Joe Thompson has been valuable. For Pam, the collegial advice and support from Marty Cohen, Gail Dykstra, and Julie Hertenstein, as well as ongoing encouragement from Mary Cay Levitt, has helped keep the excitement high and the process moving forward. We would also be remiss if we did not mention the technical advice Stew received from Nick Nonno and Bob Stone. Last, although never least, both of us sincerely value the contributions our colleague Paul Gustavson has made to us and to this book.

Our families have also been sources of great support and inspiration as we moved through this process. Special acknowledgment goes out to our spouses, Pat Liff and Rick Posey: This would have been a much more difficult and lonely process without their love, energy, support, and commitment. Finally, we wish to acknowledge all of the people out there who are trying to improve their workplaces, their performance, and themselves in an increasingly complex and challenging world. Keep up the good work, and don't forget to get visual!

Seeing Is Believing

CHAPTER 1

Imagine! A New Kind of Workplace

Have you ever wondered what it would be like to manage and be part of an organization that really works? Do you know what such an organization looks like, or how it feels to be in that kind of workplace? Have you ever had days when you wondered whether anyone in your organization really understands what your business is about? Do the people around you keep their heads down, work in seeming isolation, and appear not to understand the full performance requirements of the system? If any of this sounds familiar, you are not alone.

Have you occasionally thought about why you bother to come in to the office some days, given the number of people who just don't seem to care about the business or its results? Do you feel as though you spend too much time trying to figure out how to motivate the people around you? Do you sometimes get discouraged and feel that you are trying to carry the load by yourself? Do you wonder where all the good, energetic, and committed people are? If so, you are in good company.

Have you ever looked around your physical workplace and wondered why nothing there ever seems to change? Do you always seem to see the same furniture, the same color walls and carpet, the same photos and messages on bulletin boards? Do you even notice when new memos are posted or when information is updated? Does this familiarity create a comfort zone at the expense of a vibrancy and energy that could help channel people's efforts in more positive directions? Or have you given up on the idea that your workplace could become a new and different environment in which to spend time? We hear similar concerns from people in nearly every workplace we visit, and we have shown them, as we will show you, that workplaces do not have to be like this.

■ Imagine!

Imagine an organization that is a work of art, one that uses all the effective management tools and also the tools of an artist to produce an environment that is designed to work great. Imagine a vision statement that is more than just a bunch of words, one that captures the mission, vision, and guiding principles of the organization with a compelling image on a single page. Imagine a physical plant that is bright, airy, and open, one that has the most effective work flow and a workspace that allows people to both concentrate on their individual tasks and work together as a team. Imagine a workplace in which the walls, floors, and ceilings are decorated with a coordinated set of pictures, sculptures, banners, flags, and other displays that are all designed to link people directly to the organization's mission. Imagine that the employees are so proud of the workplace of which they are a part that they bring their families to see it. Imagine a workplace that is so visually coherent that it can instantly shape the impression or point of view of the outside world the minute a visitor enters. Visually, this would be a place that is special, a place that is filled with innovation and creativity.

Now imagine that same workplace as a place in which information is shared to an unprecedented degree, and shared with all employees in many different forms. Imagine that the employees in the organization know and understand the metrics and performance measures, and are working together as a group to try to achieve them. Imagine that the performance of the units and individual employees is posted, that all employees know exactly how they are doing relative to everybody else, that there are mechanisms in place to help low performers improve, and that high-performing teams and individuals are rewarded accordingly. Imagine a work environment in which people are celebrated in employee galleries that display photos of individuals and work teams, of the union leadership, of employee events, and of new and even former employees. Imagine that these galleries also contain photos of the families of employees. This would be an environment in which employees truly felt appreciated by their employer. Now imagine that this same environment is so compelling and so attractive that it enables the organization to recruit and retain top-notch talent. This would truly be a focused and effective workplace.

Finally, imagine that all of these different elements are brought together in one organization using modern management principles, organizational system design principles, and all the tools at the disposal of an artist. Imagine that the result is an organization in which employees are directly connected to the mission, in which information of all types is widely shared, in which employees consistently deliver top performance, in which employees feel celebrated and valued, and in which people have fun working. This is what visual management does, and this is what visual management can do in your organization. Now imagine that you can truly make this happen.

What is it that you want to see, feel, and do when you go to work? Have you made attempts to focus the efforts of people in your organization on common goals? Have you thought about how you might change from a scenario of complacency and build an effective, efficient, and fun (yes, fun!) workplace for yourself and others? If you are asking these questions of yourself, then this book is for you. Throughout the book, we share with you important lessons in how to reenergize, revitalize, and refocus your organization so that it works at its very best. We will show you a process for organizational improvement that encourages people to become more proficient, more committed, and more focused on attaining the goals of the organization. We will walk you through this process step-by-step, and we will show you how to guarantee performance improvements as a result of your efforts. We will show you how to do this across an entire organization or simply within your area or department. And we will help you do this by utilizing leading-edge management practice combined with the tools of an artist to produce a workplace that is deliberately designed to work great. In fact, we will introduce you to the art of visual management.

■ What Is Visual Management?

Visual management is a system for organizational improvement that can be used in almost any type of organization to focus attention on what is important and to improve performance across the board. It adds a new dimension to the processes, systems, and structures that make up the existing organization by utilizing strong graphic visualization techniques to heighten its focus on performance. This innovative management system adds visible and visual depth and consistency to an organization's messages about its mission and goals; it keeps information about the mission, goals, and performance in front of employees at all times; and it does this in the most visual way possible by converting information about the company, its customers, and its performance into graphic displays that cannot be ignored. Visual management appeals directly to the high level of visual literacy that exists among today's workforce.

The People–Performance Link

At its most basic, visual management establishes and reinforces a direct link between people and performance in organizations. It concentrates on aligning performance with the mission, vision, and strategies of the firm in order to ensure that the end results match what was desired at the beginning. Just imagine motivating people in your organization to attain performance improvements like these:

❏ 30 percent improvement in customer satisfaction
❏ 33 percent reduction in rework

❑ 25 percent improvement in overall productivity

❑ 20 percent improvement in accuracy

Real organizations have done this with visual management. And these are only a few examples of the performance improvements reported by organizations like those described in this book that are using visual management. What we have learned over time is that there are a number of results that can be anticipated as organizations adopt visual management.

Anticipated Outcomes of Visual Management

Productivity improvements are typical. In a visual management environment, each employee becomes actively accountable for her performance in terms of building expertise through training or education, applying that knowledge on the job, and ensuring that she is performing up to expectation. Skill matrices keep people abreast of what skills they have mastered and which ones they need to improve upon. Performance results are posted at the organization, unit, and individual level to ensure that everyone knows how the performance results are achieved. Low performers are encouraged in positive ways to improve, and they are given an incentive to do this. Results become transparent in a visual management system, and it becomes easier to identify gaps in the process and address them quickly.

Costs are typically reduced, often through increased awareness of controllable costs and reductions in rework. Employees who know exactly what is expected of them, who are well trained to deliver, and who know how they are performing at every given moment tend to focus their work effort on doing things well. Those who are given straightforward cost information and taught how to use it pay more attention to the costs that they can control and tend to reduce scrap and other waste. As a result, they improve the quality of their work output and reduce costs at the same time. There is less non-value-added work being done, and the result is greater efficiency and effectiveness.

The ability to serve the customer rises, often dramatically, in organizations that use visual management. You will read in this book about organizations that turned their cultures around through visual management, and helped their employees truly understand who the customers were and what they needed. By connecting employees to the organization's mission and customers, visual management helps organizations become more sensitive to customer needs, helps them find new ways to meet those needs, and enhances overall customer satisfaction. Employees who understand what customers need often go the extra step to take care of those customers. Perhaps as important, though, is the fact that these same employees no longer waste their time and energy on issues that are not important to the customers.

The use of modern visual learning techniques improves the knowledge, skills, and abilities of employees, as they learn and retain information more quickly and easily if it is delivered visually, at least in part. Those who have learned well the first time will make fewer errors as a result. Accuracy typically improves, as does the completion of tasks. Those who will not or cannot learn and those who will not or cannot improve are easily identified so that their performance issues can be dealt with before they become a significant challenge. Visual management clearly addresses performance challenges in organizations.

Employee satisfaction also rises in a visual management environment. People want to be part of a winning team. When they see that an organization is actively engaged in a major improvement effort that includes them, when they begin to see the positive impact of this effort, and when they begin to feel that their contributions count, their outlook on work and the organization typically changes accordingly. They become more engaged in and committed to the work, and their overall satisfaction level increases. On another level, employees in visual management organizations tend to be grateful that performance problems are finally being addressed. The employees all understand how they are doing relative to the goals and their peers, and they all understand that action will be taken if poor performers do not improve, so there are few surprises and relatively fewer grievances.

When an organization adopts a performance-based reward and recognition system that is consistent with visual management principles, the overall credibility of the system naturally rises. Many organizations, over the years, have adopted reward and recognition systems that have no teeth: They are not based on measurable performance or controllable elements. This can result in complaints of unfairness or cronyism. It is difficult to be cynical, however, about a system that is based on data that employees get to see and can control, one in which employees are rewarded on the basis of preset goals that are directly linked to the organization's goals, and one in which they know and understand the operation of the system.

In tight labor markets, visual management organizations tend to have better opportunities to recruit new employees. Prospective employees are attracted to the culture, the physical plant, and the growing reputation for success that these organizations develop.

Of course, there is also the improved physical space, which is the most obvious, although not the most important, outcome of visual management. Physical space is used in an optimum fashion, work flow is enhanced and supported by reconfigurations of space, and wasted space is eliminated. Workplaces tend to become brighter, better organized around work and people, and more functional. They look better than before, constantly reinforce the mission, and remind employees every minute of why they are there. All of this helps support productivity improvements.

Managers often tell us that this all sounds great, but they don't really grasp what's different. They have struggled throughout their careers to lead and motivate employees, to get people to pay attention to the right things, and to improve results. Some are concerned that they won't know what to do or how to manage in a visual management environment; more are concerned that they wouldn't know such an environment if they tripped over it. We know otherwise. As managers learn more about this process, they find that it makes sense to them on an intellectual and emotional level, and they become hooked on visual management.

How Do You Know That You Are in a Visual Management Organization?

The easiest way to know that you are in a visual management organization is simply by looking around. In many organizations, the mission, vision, and guiding principles are printed on a piece of paper or a business card and given out to the employees. At best, employees will glance at the paper once or twice, then put it away and rarely refer to it again. It does not make a lasting impression on them, and the power that a clear mission or vision statement can have is lost to the organization. Sometimes you will see a mission statement in a frame on a wall, but typically it is not located in a place where employees see it constantly, so it has little impact on them or their work. Employees in many organizations have become so focused on trying to do the work that they are required to do, and to retain their jobs in the face of downsizing and the export of jobs overseas, that the mission doesn't seem real. In addition, we often find that the work environment supports this lack of emphasis on mission, and even downplays the customer focus that has become central to so many organizations today.

We also see cookie-cutter work environments that look modern and efficient, but that all have the same look and feel. It seems that a telephone center looks like a telephone center no matter where it is located. Unless you see the names on the doors, it can be difficult to know whether you are in a law firm, an accounting firm, or a marketing firm. And you may know that you are in a paper mill or an auto parts factory, but can you tell which company owns it or what differentiates it from its competitors? Although common designs may be efficient, they are not distinctive in any way, and they usually are not stimulating work environments. We are not sure who ever decreed that all organizations of a particular type should look the same, but we disagree strenuously.

From the moment you walk into a visual management environment, you are struck by how different it looks and feels from most other places you have been. Pictures, posters, banners, and other visual displays tell you immediately that someone has worked hard to set the tone of this organization. You are greeted with clear information about the organization's mission and vision that is displayed using a variety of media. You quickly recognize that this organization is customer focused, and often you know instantly who the customers are from the displays and photographs. You also see lots of evidence that employees are valued here and are considered a critical asset.

As you look more closely, you begin to see other things. The displays show a dedication and a commitment to the mission that is often missing elsewhere. You may even see a degree of creativity that is more often attributed to museums and their display spaces than to work environments. You begin to realize that the entire organization appears to be a cohesive work of art that could be put together only through the joint efforts of many people.

Once you get over the attention-grabbing power of the visual displays, you begin to notice the information displays. In visual management organizations, performance goals and objectives are displayed in a clear and recognizable manner, in many different forms, and in many different places. You further note that this information is there for all to see, rather than being treated as confidential or eyes-only. Finally, you observe that the goals and objectives are clearly defined, highly visible, and creatively displayed, and visual displays mounted around the facility show you that the goals and objectives are directly linked to rewards. The visuals tell you that the employees here are as engaged in performance improvement efforts and management of the organization as are its actual managers.

As you take a step back, you may be a bit overwhelmed by how all encompassing visual management can be. Every aspect of space in a visual management organization is used for two primary purposes: to connect employees to the mission and to make sure that the organization achieves its optimum performance. Employees' connection to the mission provides guidance for their work activities and is important to performance improvement, and the link is made explicit through the use of powerful visual images that reinforce this connection. As you examine the individual displays in detail, you slowly realize that they are all closely connected, and that they are all designed to support and improve the bottom line. You realize that the desired outcomes are being achieved through an integrated combination of sound and workable management, organization design, and fine arts principles. You actually begin to see the links and connections that make these organizations work better. And that's how you can tell that you are in a visual management organization.

■ What Does It Take to Do Visual Management?

The commitment to doing visual management is a significant one for any organization. Visual management is a process that focuses on developing a critical link between a carefully defined mission, a set of operating systems and structures that align with that mission, and the desired performance outcomes of an organization. It can be undertaken as a complete process in which the organization reviews and revises its mission and structure. It can also be implemented as an overlay to an existing organization design and effective operating systems, although in this case its success is directly linked to the soundness of these elements. Hence, an organization that is considering visual management must review, and often refine, its systems and structures as part of the implementation process. Successful implementation of visual management requires top management commitment, strong leadership, expertise in a variety of disciplines, varying levels of resources, and enthusiasm and energy from within the organization. It is a long-term commitment to changing an organization's culture with a goal of sustained improvement.

What's in It for Us?

Organizationally, there is a great deal to be gained from visual management. As you will see in the stories that follow in this book, companies that have implemented visual management have achieved significant performance improvements, strengthened work flows, and improved employee relations in general. An organization that can align its mission, vision, strategies, and goals with its functional capabilities has moved a step closer to performance improvement. If that organization can take these aligned strategies and systems and show workers exactly what they need to do, how they need to do it, and what level of performance is required to meet the goals, then it will develop a culture of success. If, further, the organization can find ways to celebrate employees and their contributions to the desired outcomes, then people will become more committed to its success each day. Thus, the organization improves productivity by building a direct focus on performance, improves customer satisfaction through heightened awareness of what customers really need and want, reduces costs by removing waste from the system, creates a culture of performance, and supports employee commitment.

At the unit level, visual management brings a clearer focus to the contributions that the department or unit has made to overall organizational results. The department can define its contribution to the goals of the organization more precisely, translate that contribution into performance targets at both unit and individual levels, and focus attention on meeting those targets. Although a single department cannot expect to realize the full benefits that come from complete organizational alignment, we do see almost immediate performance improvements and a clearer understanding of what is important on the part of employees when visual management is implemented at the unit level. Moreover, people begin to notice that something is different and successful here and begin to gravitate toward that unit.

At the individual level, visual management brings two critical contributions. First, it keeps the organization's mission and goals in front of people at all times, leaving no room for misunderstanding or inattention. It provides a clarity of purpose that keeps people working on the right things. Second, it focuses great attention on group and individual performance, helping people to understand where they are doing well and where they need to improve. It takes the surprises out of performance review by providing all employees with consistent and very frequent performance feedback. At the same time, it celebrates employees' accomplishments and shows them how valuable they are to the organization. For individuals in the organization, visual management brings greater awareness of their actual performance, shows them that they are expected to deliver what they were hired to deliver, and keeps them focused on learning and improving their skills in order to improve their performance. It builds stronger leaders and managers with this focus on performance and the development of structures and systems to better manage people and performance. In essence, if an organization has the will and develops the skill to implement visual management, it can reap the benefits for itself and for its people.

How Long Will It Take?

Visual management, like many significant changes in organizations, is an ongoing process rather than a static program. Some results may be seen in as little as two or three months, although the major performance gains take longer. In general, however, we would anticipate that after two or three months, the mission and vision will have been clarified and developed visually for everyone in the organization to see. We would also expect that a review of the organization's structure and operating systems would be well under way. If adjustments are required here, we may need to spend another one to six months dealing with the needed changes, depending on the degree of change necessary.

At the end of the first year, an organization should see a number of changes and improvements. First, its operating systems and structures will be in better alignment, working in a synchronized and cohesive way and assuring that all activities will be focused in a common direction toward the same goals and initiatives. The workforce, too, will be more focused on its mission and usually will exhibit more energy and excitement about the work and the workplace. The physical plant typically will have undergone dramatic improvement, and the work flow will have become more efficient and more effective as a result. Communication and information-sharing activities will have improved, there will be more and better information available throughout the organization, and more effective communication mechanisms will be in use. Also, there will be greater management and employee accountability as a result of the increased focus on performance and learning. Finally, there will be a significant change in the way the organization works to continually improve its performance and enhance its culture: These activities will have become embedded in the way the organization works on a day-to-day basis and will no longer be a new change directive.

The total amount of time required to implement and fine-tune a visual management system is usually two to three years. The bulk of the work typically occurs in the first year to eighteen months, although renewal activities are initiated as soon as the system is substantially in place. The differences in the length of time needed by different organizations stem from each organization's initial degree of readiness, the skill of the people involved, the organization's commitment of resources to the process, the size of the organization, and the degree of change required and planned for.

How Much Will It Cost?

The cost of a visual management implementation varies widely, depending on the same criteria as the timing. The longer it takes to implement visual management, the more it may cost. In Chapter 7, we show that some organizations have implemented this system for less than $50,000, whereas others have spent upward of $300,000 to $400,000. In some cases, the funding comes totally from internal resources; in others, benefactors and other outside supporters come forward to contribute once they see the initial progress. So, the answer to how much it will cost depends on how much there is to do and what level of resource commitment is available. Most organizations can find creative ways to raise funds for the actual visuals, and many already have some budget set aside for improvement projects. Over the long run, we have seen that visual management pays for itself through the performance improvements and reduced turnover that result from a successful process.

How Much Time Is Lost? Won't Performance Decrease in the Short Run?

There is no reason that performance has to be negatively affected in the short run by a visual management implementation. Unlike many change efforts, visual management does not take a group of people offline for many months to conduct detailed studies and analyses. It does not require any group of people to dedicate all of their work hours to the transition process. Moreover, it does not require that the organization engage in a massive education or retraining program that diverts precious resources away from the mission. Certainly, some education about visual management is required, and employees who are not performing as expected will sometimes need retraining to build or strengthen their skills. But the overall commitment of time by any group or individual is modest, and most of this time is typically spent on improving skills for improved performance.

Isn't This Just Another Flavor-of-the-Month Program?

Visual management is not a system that can be selected randomly or lightly. It requires a significant commitment of knowledge, leadership, and planning. It is customized for each and every adopting organization, and it is designed to meet the specific needs of each organization. Visual management has specific goals and targets, and progress toward those goals and targets can be measured at each step of the way. Because it involves the whole organization or unit, it has been designed to have systemwide impact, and it is difficult for people to hide from the process. Once it is under way, it does not go away because a few individuals have decided to ignore it.

Visual management is not a magic bullet that will cure all of an organization's ills. It does not promise exceptional short-term improvements based on untested or unsupported management theories. Instead, visual management is a process that draws upon the strengths of tried-and-true management systems that are integrated with the fine arts in order to support and improve an organization's ability to focus clearly on performance improvement. The visual changes are often dramatic, and the ultimate performance improvements are exciting to see, although the cultural changes are sometimes subtle initially. Once it is under way, however, the process becomes a self-fulfilling prophecy and continues growing as long as it has top-level support and some degree of resource commitment. The benefits of visual management are too significant and too striking for it to be treated as a flavor-of-the-month program.

■ How This Book Is Organized

This book has been designed to introduce you to the concept and practice of visual management. It describes the process, tells of the real-life experiences of a variety of organizations that are engaged in visual management implementations, and serves as a guide to help you determine whether visual management is appropriate for you and your organization. It provides a lot more detail to flesh out the brief summary responses offered in this introduction. Ultimately, we hope this book helps you and your organization to find new and better ways to focus on performance improvement and reinforce a culture that supports your mission.

We start in Chapter 2 by explaining why being visual is so important in today's work environments. We look at how societal and technological changes have affected people and work, at the changing characteristics of the workforce, and at the changing ways in which people learn. We then show the implications of these changes for organizations and describe the importance of the need for organizations to work better.

Chapter 3 explores the foundations of visual management and discusses where it came from. We look at leadership, culture, and management practice to show how lessons from these areas have been incorporated into visual management. We also show the contribution of systems thinking and organization design to this process. Finally, we explore for you the fine arts link, introducing you to some basic fine arts concepts and describing their importance in visual management.

Chapter 4 introduces you to several visual management organizations and uses information and photos from them to illustrate the major elements of visual management. In this chapter, we describe the physical settings, the changes that were implemented, and some of the impacts of visual management on the organizations and their people. We look at four different types of organizations: manufacturing, government, health care, and education. This chapter shows what visual management can do in real organizations.

In Chapters 5 and 6, we provide a road map and a plan for developing and implementing visual management in your organization. These chapters take you step-by-step through the six phases of the visual management planning and implementation process. At each step, we highlight key concerns and activities and identify the questions that you should ask in order to gather the right information for planning and decision making. In addition, we share with you the anticipated results from each phase of the process. By the end of Chapter 6, you should have a solid understanding of what visual management is and what it is not, as well as the process for bringing it into your organization.

Finally, in Chapter 7, we help you assess whether visual management is right for you and your organization. We show you what it takes to lead a successful implementation, and we try to keep you focused on the goals of such a process. We explain the high points and the challenges of the system, and we highlight the benefits of selecting visual management as a way of life. As you read this book, we ask you to keep in mind that visual management is not just about creating another pretty face. It is a system that is primarily about performance results. Just imagine what it can do for you and your organization.

CHAPTER 2

Why Visual Is Important

The world of work today is unlike the world of work that our parents or their parents faced. Before the introduction of automation and robotics, our assembly lines moved at a slower pace; before the advances in telecommunications, we discussed problems and their solutions face-to-face; before the Internet became widely available, we worked in physical teams rather than virtual teams; and before we became part of a globally interconnected economy, we could still manage much of the information that came our way within our own companies. Just as robotics, telecommunications, and computer technology have changed the face of work, they have also changed the way in which people gather, interpret, and make sense of the information around them. Today, the means by which people deal with information rely heavily on visual cues for the proper and rapid transmission and receipt of messages.

Have you wondered whatever happened to the days of steady growth, predictable change, and manageable transition? Or are you one of the generation who wonders what older workers and managers are talking about when they discuss moving an organization forward sequentially, one step at a time? Are you a technological dinosaur, or are you a person who grew up with computers, PDAs, and cell phones? Do you remember the first television in your neighborhood, or do you still wonder how people can manage without multiscreen receivers and cable or satellite transmission? Is change something that you worry about, or is it such a natural part of your life that you take it for granted? Are you a member of the GI Generation or the Silent Generation, born before 1945, whose life experiences were influenced heavily by economic hardship and world war? Or are you a Baby Boomer, born between 1946 and 1964 and raised in an era of postwar idealism and massive social change? How about a member of the Thirteenth Generation, including Gen X and Gen Y: born between 1965 and 1985 and reacting to massive technological and economic growth and change? Or are you a Millennial, born after 1985 into an increasingly complex and global economy and society?[1] Are you part of the MTV Generation? The Pepsi Generation? We seem to have adopted such labels from popular social culture to identify and describe sets of common characteristics among age or experience cohorts in the United States.

Workplaces today are staffed with individuals who represent the entire spectrum of such characteristics, people who make sense of the world and the work environment in quite different ways because of their background, upbringing, learning styles, and experiences on the technological innovation curve.[2] There has been, perhaps, no other time in Western history in which changes in technology have driven such diversity of practice and experience in the workplace.

Many workplaces have not kept pace with the rapid changes in communication and information-sharing technology that have created significant differences in how we send and receive information. There is so much information available, there is so much detail in what is available, and there are so many ways in which to communicate it that many organizations have become paralyzed as they try to decide how and what to do to get good information to their employees. Many err on the side of opening the books completely, nearly drowning employees in oceans of numbers and financial statements; others give only highlights that do not tell employees enough about what is really happening. They struggle to find good ways in which to support workers who are trying to succeed amid the deluge of information and the demands for greater and greater performance. Yet, despite the fact that significant changes in communication and information-sharing patterns have affected how people learn about their work, how and what they communicate at work, and with whom they communicate, these organizations are not utilizing optimum communication and information-sharing techniques to their advantage. All of this, of course, has an impact on performance.

We have become a visual society in fast-paced times. In all facets of life, information is shared through some form of visual media. Radio today, despite its strength as a medium for information sharing, entertainment, and talk shows, is often used to provide background noise for other activities, except in those locations where television transmission is not adequate. Television, in addition to everything else it does, has created the equivalent of video radio with music channels and music videos. Even telephones are going visual with the advent of new cell technology and the videophone. Virtually all of the technology that we have come to depend upon for communication and information sharing is visual in nature, and the visual cues generated by today's technology provide information and saturate that information with meaning. Combined with this move to visual cuing is a trend toward single-image and split-second information sharing, which can be done most easily with visual images. To understand the increased pace and significant reliance on visual cues and messages today, we need to look at sociocultural change in the United States.

■ Picking Up the Pace

Think about the social, cultural, and technological leaps forward in the past fifty years. In the 1950s, we got our news and entertainment from newspapers and radio; television was not yet widespread and remained primarily black and white until the 1960s; music was played from record albums or 45s (we refer to these as vinyl today); many homes with telephones still had party lines, and few long-distance calls were ever made from home; and quantitative data were collated by hand and summarized using primitive adding machines with columns of numbered keys. By the mid- to late 1960s, more than 90 percent of households had televisions, with television rapidly approaching the saturation level of radio;[3] music was available on eight-track tapes as well as albums; computers were enormous physical systems designed for the exclusive use of large, wealthy businesses; telegrams were still a standard form of international communication; and we had begun to advance to ten-key calculators for personal use. We had only a few television channels, and only a couple of newspapers were readily available in any given area because physical circulation was limited. Leisure travel was primarily by train and automobile, giving travelers time to see and absorb new sights.

In the 1950s and into the early 1960s, the pace of life was relatively slow, and we had time to absorb information and process its implications. Changes were logical, sequential, and often predictable. This was the era of William H. Whyte's "organization man"[4]: middle-class line and staff workers who felt that they belonged to their organizations even though they had little control over their direction or their future. It was a time in which Americans really learned to become members of and contributors to organization life and began to define themselves, in part, by their organizational roles.

The Beginnings of Rapid Change

By the 1970s, however, life had begun to change in earnest, and quickly. By then, nearly all households had televisions, and color television was rapidly replacing black-and-white technology. The number of television stations in the United States was growing faster than the number of radio stations, and rapid adoption of cable television with as many as a dozen channels had begun. Our news came in hour-long programs, reported by well-informed, articulate anchors who reported the highlights of news around the world. Instead of a single focus on America, we learned to pay attention to what was happening around the globe.

Advances in miniaturization allowed us to develop smaller computers and tape recorder/players, party line telephones disappeared except in the most rural areas, and communication technology began to really advance. Daily newspaper circulation began a slow decline in the 1970s that has continued into the 2000s; this may be related to the increased television saturation in the American household, which certainly has contributed to the growing dependence on visual images in the United States.

By the 1980s, telephones, radios, and televisions had reached nearly full market saturation in American households. Cable television was growing rapidly, and the VCR was catching on. We became plugged in and turned on, and the ways in which information was shared in this country began to change even more rapidly. New segments of the economy opened up, increased communication capability opened wider service segments than were possible before, and our transition to a service-based economy began.

Throughout the 1980s, we saw exceptional changes in communication methods and even more significant changes in message content. Daily newspaper circulation remained in a steady, slow decline, and consolidation in the industry reduced the number of newspapers published. Desktop computers speeded up our writing and editing processes as well as making it easier to collect, collate, and manipulate large masses of data more quickly. Technological advances in information processing and communication created the capacity for greater speed in developing and dispersing news and other information. The pace continued to quicken. Companies fought to keep up in an increasingly global environment: Not only did they have to deal with domestic communication and information sharing; they also had to deal with the cross-cultural challenges to effective communication created by the new global marketplace. Globalization raised the bar on developing effective communication strategies and information-sharing practices, and most organizations could not keep pace with the required changes.

The Explosion of Rapid Change

From 1990 through the turn of the century, change exploded exponentially. The growth of cellular technology skyrocketed. People were suddenly connected to one another without being connected to a land base, allowing information to be shared from remote physical locations at all times of the day or night. In addition, satellite and other non-cable-delivered premium television systems had become available and were making significant inroads into the massive cable market, though it, too, was still growing. It seems that the proliferation of broadcast channels available through satellite and cable was more directly responsible for creating a generation of "channel surfers" than was the remote control, which had been around since the mid-1950s. Television programming also expanded rapidly; a plethora of commercials continually bombarded viewers of commercial television, and we learned to surf multiple channels simultaneously in order to take in more information and entertainment at one sitting. Information became available instantly, and we lived history in the moment in which it happened. We knew a lot more about markets, organizations, and business because of the advances in media technology and availability, and there were many more sources of information than we had ever been able to access in the past. Our sensory overload was just beginning.

The nature of play and gaming also changed dramatically during this period, and we entered the era of video arcades, handheld game units, and home-based electronic gaming technology. Technology has moved light-years from the earliest video game, Pong, which is laughable by today's standards because of its slow speed and single target, to the complex interactive games of today. This era of interactive video gaming and interactive learning technology, in which we can learn to fly, program a computer, explore unknown territories, or search out unheard-of fantasy lands from the comfort of our own homes, creates even more stimuli contributing to information overload.

In addition, computer and Internet use grew exponentially during the decade-plus since 1990. The Internet gave us access to massive amounts of information and pushed us to read, digest, and learn faster than ever before. The use of high-speed broadband Internet service nearly doubled between August 2000 and September 2001.[5] With such rapid growth, these technologies have become commonplace in our personal and our work lives, increasing both the amount of information available to us and the speed with which it is accessible. They have also increased our reliance on visual information. There is virtually no type of information that we cannot access today if we have the appropriate technology. The average worker in the United States has significantly more information about his company at his fingertips than ever before in history, and much of that information comes from outside the organization in which he works. Workers who want to know what the competition is doing need only search the Internet for the information they seek. Technology has created a generation of information hounds who expect access to lots of information whenever they want it. These changes are astounding and have had a significant impact on people and work.

Music, too, has changed over the past five decades. In the United States, we have evolved from a fascination with rock and roll and the Beatles through a stage in which disco was the hot sound and then on to a fascination with acid rock, hip-hop, and rap. Traditional country-and-western music has been enhanced with amplified sound, a greater array of instruments, and even crossover hits. New releases are accompanied by music videos, creating a multisensory experience from what was once only an audio one. With each passing decade, the beat of most music, no matter what the category, has become faster, and the volume has increased. All facets of media and the arts have been changing, becoming more complex, moving more quickly, and creating more and more stimuli to which people have had to respond. Even here, the pace has quickened, pushing us to move even faster.

Changes in Technology and Their Results

The changes wrought in information and communication systems in the United States during the last fifty years are staggering. We moved from radio to satellite transmission for television, from hand-dialed, hard-wired telephone sets to voice-command visual cellular technology, from huge multibuilding computer systems that read keypunched cards to large, slow desktop computers to microcomputers that fit into a pocket. Audio- and videotapes gave way to CDs and DVDs, cellular technology created significant competition for more traditional telecommunications, cable television was given a run for its money by satellite companies, and the world evolved into an interconnected global network. As Figure 2-1 shows, in less than two decades, cable television use grew by more than 50 percent, VCR penetration more than quadrupled, and the use of cellular technology grew from zero to about 140 million users in the United States alone; these trends were accompanied by a slow decline in newspaper circulation as people moved toward the visual and audio communication formats.

During this same period, organizations have become larger and more complex, with simple structures giving way to matrix frameworks and global networks. Greater collaboration and interconnection make the sharing of accurate and timely information imperative. With this increase in the complexity of organizations comes an increased need to focus on performance, and performance data have become as complex as our organization designs. Information technology has provided rapid collation and reporting techniques to help us make sense of these complex data. Yet, we often have not done a very good job of sorting the data into chunks and segments that are immediately useful to those who need them.

Think about how people today gather information and make decisions with it compared to prior generations. Assume, for example, that there is a problem with parts supply for an assembly operation. In the 1960s and 1970s, we might have had to stop the line, send a message up the chain of command to an individual who was empowered to contact the supplier by telephone to find out what the problem was, and then formulate a solution. Information about that solution would then be passed back down the line, a time-consuming process. Today, in many plants, operators have the necessary technology and are empowered to contact the supplier directly, often by online computer technology. Issues are resolved more quickly and at the point at which they occur.

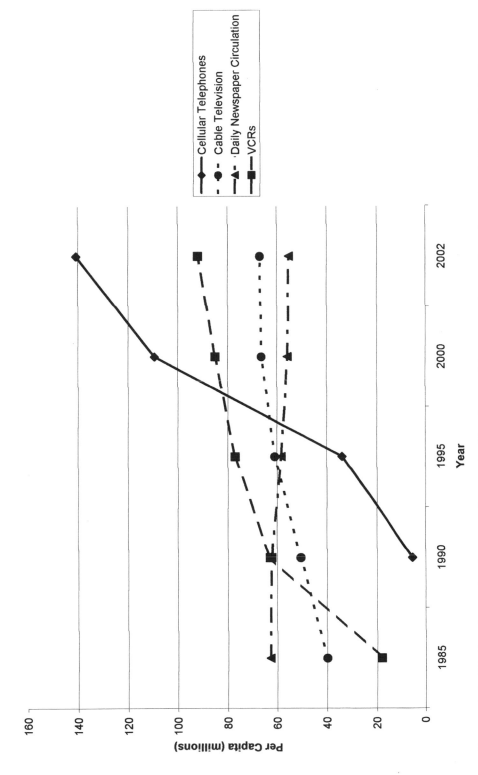

Figure 2-1. Technological advances dramatically changed how people send and receive information in just two decades.

Consider the evolution of teamwork also. Before the introduction of meeting software that could handle virtual meetings with participants in locations spanning the globe, physical proximity was considered to be a critical requirement for effective teams in organizations. Teleconferencing, instant messaging, chat rooms dedicated to particular teams, and intranet and Internet technologies have shrunk geographic dispersion and cut across time and datelines to allow real-time work and collaboration. When problems occur or projects require attention, more people, from more places, are able to get involved very quickly and at the same time. We are becoming accustomed to this kind of speed and virtual proximity in today's technologically driven environment.

With the advent of this information and technology age, society has been confronted with an exponential increase in information-sharing methods and mechanisms that have affected every facet of life at work, at home, and at play. This has introduced added stress and confusion into both the workplace and the home, and it complicates an already complex culture of work. We have kept up with all of this by giving up depth for breadth.

◼ The Impact of Speed: Overload

In this interconnected world, we are bombarded with information everywhere we turn. We start up our computer systems, open our e-mail, and are confronted with fifty to one hundred messages each day. We sort through offers for mortgages, offers to help us spy on others' Internet habits, offers for products and services we may never have known existed, and requests for information along with the business requests. Some of this information is relevant to what we are doing, and some is not. Yet we have to battle our way through the barrage to find what we need. Instant messages pop up on our monitors if we have not installed blocking software, and we can conduct live chats on-screen as we engage in other activities. Multitasking has become a required behavior; multimedia transmission of information (including visual media) has become an expectation rather than a surprise. We are giving up telephone modems for DSL technology on our home computers because a 56K download is no longer fast enough for data or information. As shown in Figure 2-2, household access to computers has grown rapidly, as has Internet access.

In terms of processor speed, we have seen a dramatic change since the 1970s, when the Apple II computer worked at what was then a blistering pace of 1 MHz. Today, we commonly use personal computers whose processors run at speeds of 2.4 GHz and above. As we have become accustomed to the faster processors, we have demanded more from them, thus adding even more pressure to do more and do it faster. We are expected to read and interpret messages quickly, and the visual cues in these messages are increasingly important. We use action figures, flashing lights, moving arrows, and other visual devices to grab people's attention so that they will get the message quickly and succinctly.

Today, when we turn on a television, we find an incredible variety of information. Some of it is pure entertainment, some is pure commercial, and some is twenty-four hours per day, seven days per week news or politics. We even have a new language that has grown up with the advent and explosive growth of cable and satellite television: Docudramas and infomercials, which were unheard of twenty years ago, are commonplace, and more time seems to be spent in commercial breaks than on actual programs today. The two or three major television networks of yesterday have ballooned into hundreds of channels, and channel surfing in order to keep up with this explosion of sensory input seems to have become a national pastime.

If one looks around the business section of an aircraft or scans people in a waiting room or on some form of public transportation today, it seems that more people are getting their news from *USA Today* than from the *Los Angeles Times,* the *San Francisco Chronicle,* the *New York Times,* or the *Washington Post*. Some people lament that we have become a nation that reads only headlines and brief synopses of news stories. Many point and click on a computer rather than read periodicals and books in a library. We take in information in a series

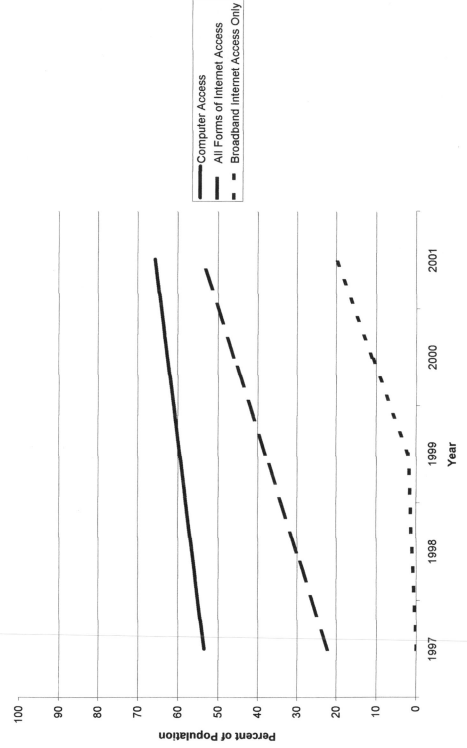

Figure 2-2. Growing computer and Internet use means that communication relies increasingly on visual imaging.

of brief sound bites rather than through in-depth reading and research. We often have no choice, since information comes at us so
quickly, and we have learned to adapt to the staccato pace.

Images Come at Dizzying Speed

We watch films on our own large-screen televisions, and these films
provide more images in their opening scenes than older films provided in their entire length. Compare, for example, the opening scene
from the 1998 film *Saving Private Ryan* with the invasion of Normandy as shown in 1962's *The Longest Day*. In *Saving Private Ryan*,
we are confronted with images that come at us with dizzying speed,
the result of editing that creates a bombardment of images and sound
to grab us and focus us instantly. We are there in the midst of the
horror of the invasion of Normandy. Compared to this reality, *The
Longest Day* makes the same invasion seem like a slow walk in the
park. We have also given up the careful and often time-consuming
process of detailed character development used in earlier films and
replaced it with the staccato of action scene piled upon action scene.
Films today typically allow fast-paced and complex special effects to
tell the story rather than have the story develop through the principal
characters. We have become conditioned to understand the complexity of the stories and capture their meaning through these visual effects rather than through slower-paced character development. Our
leisure activities thus reinforce the growing pattern of fast visual interpretation for information gathering.

Even recreation is attached to power sources and headphones
today. We exercise differently, watching television as we ride exercise
bicycles and listening to CDs as we jog. Our automobiles have video
players and interactive GPS systems that provide visual driving directions for us. From the time they are able to hold an electronic game
in their hands, children play interactive games with characters that
move and demand responses at mind-boggling speeds. They are enam-
ored with action figures and are captivated by the ability to control
them in action. Video games toss images at players at an incredible

pace, accompanied by pounding music, contributing to our expectation that life will be lived at high speed. We learn to react in split seconds, and we expect the next game or information download to be as mesmerizing and as fast as the games and information with which we have already become familiar. If the games don't move quickly enough or the modem speed is too slow, we become bored and change games or activities.

Sometimes, even if a game manages to capture and retain our attention, we trade it in for something else very quickly. Marketing and advertising messages exhort us to buy the newest version, to trade in our current product for the latest model, and to continue to demand the newest version as soon as it is available. We no longer assume that products are developed with some type of long-term built-in obsolescence and that we may have to replace them at some future date; instead, we immediately ask for the details of planned upgrades. We expect to have to change these products or trade them in almost as soon as we acquire them in order to stay current with the market. The advent of rapid downloads, faster game speeds, and nearly instant upgrades exacerbates our increasingly short attention span. Because we are surrounded by such expectations in our daily lives, we have come to expect these quick changes at work also.

People today are becoming part of the MTV Generation, whether or not they choose to do so. They have come to expect fast-paced imaging and loud, attention-grabbing noise. Back in the 1950s, a typical camera shot lasted thirty to fifty seconds; by the 1990s, one lasted about five seconds; and today, commercials often change camera shots every second or so.[6] Changing camera shots mean changes in audio input, too. Not only are we bombarded with new visual images, but these images are also enhanced and emphasized by the accompanying sound. On television, commercial messages are often broadcast at a higher decibel level than most programming. The difference in volume helps capture the viewers' attention before they change the channel, and the viewers are able to pick up information about the content of the advertisement in a split second.

In essence, we are surrounded by media that teach us that we can get the information we need in fast, succinct, focused sound bites, without having to dig for it, and these media rely to a great extent on visual images to send their messages. We are continually confronted with high-speed images and sounds that drive an overwhelming desire to be more and more informed and entertained, or an intense desire to at least be able to make sense of it all. People have become accustomed to living in sound bites, to having information predigested and handed to them in brief, rapid doses, and they carry these sensory expectations everywhere, including the workplace. According to the Associated Press, even NBC will cash in on the short attention spans of its viewers by developing sixty-second minimovies and airing them between scheduled network programs.[7]

■ Implications for the Workplace

The American workplace in general, though, has not kept up with these sociocultural changes. Instead of recognizing that today's employees accumulate information through brief and pointed sound bites, the managers of these employees make massive amounts of work-related information available in full, unexcerpted written versions. Most organizations have crafted their mission, vision, and core values statements as written documents; they have also prepared strategic, quality, or business plans in written form. In addition, many organizations have created detailed written instruction manuals covering a variety of technical issues. Employees receive position descriptions, performance standards, organization and team goals, performance data, and benefit information in written form. The sheer volume of written information is simply overwhelming to the workers who may need it the most, and it adds dramatically to information overload in the workplace.

The Impact of Overload

This overload situation causes people to tune out, to lose critical data, and to become bored with the work. The speed with which they must assess and use the information that comes to them also leads to errors and reduced performance because the information is not available in a quick, focused manner that is easy to access and interpret. The overload caused by excess information leads to a sense of having to work too hard and too fast; the speed of information downloads also adds to stress and a sense of being overwhelmed by the work.

A relatively new employee in a Midwestern phone center operation once commented that she was overwhelmed by her work. She had to answer the telephone, quickly provide service information with which she was not yet familiar, and get on to the next call as soon as she possibly could. "It's not the number of calls, or even the speed with which we have to take them," she said. "It's that there is so much information to sort through on my screen that I never know if I am on the right screen or answering the right question. It used to be simpler when we had different areas to deal with different information requests. But since we got these new computers, we each have access to all of the information, and we are expected to be able to use it. I go home at night with my head spinning from all the information I have accessed during the day. I often feel completely overloaded and overwhelmed, and I don't even know if I am doing a good job!"

Do you recall the now-famous 1952 episode of *I Love Lucy* in which Lucy and Ethel were working on a packaging line in a candy factory? The line kept speeding up until they could no longer work quickly enough to package all of the candy. They began first to eat the candy and then to hide it in order to try to keep up with the pace of the line. The scenes on the packaging line are great visual reminders of what information overload does to people today.

A recent study of work overload by the Families and Work Institute yielded interesting findings concerning the impact of overload on employees and employers. It found that three in ten employees feel chronically overworked, that this sense of overload contributes directly to work errors and to anger and frustration with the employer, and that the overload increases the likelihood of the employees seeking work with another employer. For employers, the lessons are clear:

Overloaded employees are more likely to make errors, perform at lower levels, look for other employment, and feel more stressed and less healthy than their counterparts who are not so overloaded.[8] Anything that can be done to reduce these consequences will contribute positively to the organization's future.

Loss of Connection to the Work and the Organization

It may seem obvious that employees who feel overloaded at work will take the resulting stress home with them, and that the work-life conflict they experience on the job will affect their family and friends as well as their colleagues at work. It may not be so obvious, however, that there is both too much to assimilate and do and too little time in which to see and do it. The information overload problem is due, in part, to the speed with which information is delivered to people, as well as the sheer volume of the information delivered. A by-product of this speed and volume is a loss of meaning and of connection to the work and the people in the organization. Eventually, it may also lead to increased turnover among employees.

Decades ago, employees typically felt great loyalty to their employers; they identified with their employers and took pride in being part of their companies. Most of them believed that they would retire from the same employer with which they began their careers, and even those who knew that they would hold more than one position in more than one organization thought that they would spend many years with each employer. Sometime during the last twenty-five years, though, the perceptions of employees and employers changed. Downsizing and the migration of work outside the United States have reduced our national sense of employment stability and increased the uncertainty of long-term employment with a single employer. Movement from one organization to another forces workers to ramp up faster than ever before in order to hit the ground running in their new positions. The need for new employees to immediately understand the operations in their new surroundings places pressure on companies to find mechanisms for faster, more accurate means to get this information out to the new employees. Yet most still rely solely on the written word.

The Impact of Longer Hours

Information overload and instability/insecurity are prime factors contributing to the high stress levels of today's workforce. So are longer working hours and the decreased use of earned vacation time. In addition to increases in the actual hours worked, decreases in the use of vacation time, and a growing sense of being overworked, we find that employees are faced with longer commuting times and distances, particularly in major metropolitan areas. An increase in commute miles means increased travel time to and from work and less leisure time with family and friends. This, too, adds to the stress and overload of today's workforce. The number of on-the-job claims for stress-related illness is far above that in past generations, as people are simply overwhelmed with the pace of work and life.

Furthermore, spending an increased amount of time at work drives us to seek more and more social interactions there. We treat work time as family time and blur the distinction between the two. Business trips become family vacations, with at least one family member wearing two hats for the entire time. The stress caused by the blurring of the boundaries between work and family life also adds to our personal stress overload. We search for new meaning among the overload of information and for new connections wherever we can find them. What is happening to employees in today's workplaces suggests that we are fortunate if they can sort through the barrage of information, job demands, time constraints, and personal needs to get their jobs done. We know that such overload has a negative impact on performance.

Ways to Improve Performance

Organizations today continue to seek means for improving performance, and it seems that the adoption of systems to help employees manage and reduce this overload would be appropriate choices. If companies can find more effective ways to collect and organize critical information and disseminate that information to their employees, they will have taken a huge step toward reducing the confusion created by information overload in the workplace. Further, if the means they use to manage this process appeal to the ways in which today's employees gather and utilize information, then companies will be more successful at ensuring that the right information gets to the appropriate people. In other words, if organizations use information-sharing and communication methods that fit the expectations and learning styles of their employees, they have a greater chance of meeting their performance goals. This is precisely what visual management does.

Being visual is consistent with the spirit of the times. It appeals to a wide variety of stakeholders, uses a wide range of visual media, and takes full advantage of prevalent learning styles. Visual management helps organizations focus their employees' attention on what is important, reinforces the organization's mission and values, and gives employees all of the right information to help them improve performance. Visual management helps organize information and processes around one or more central strategic themes. It helps build synergies among operations by constantly focusing on core organizational themes and the links between them. Visual management does this by helping the organization reduce its reliance on the written word and begin to manage what people see.

■ It's Not About Just Looking Good—It's About Working Better

The sociological changes in the world of work have created a new set of social values and thought patterns in the American workplace. For those who are concerned about performance in the workplace, it will be increasingly important to understand the implications of such changes for work itself. Visual management is *not* a new social order.

It is not simply about looking good in order to appeal to today's generation of workers. It is, fundamentally, about creating workplaces that work better because they are designed with today's workers in mind. They appeal to the ways in which today's workers learn, the ways in which they gather data, and the ways in which they most easily make sense of the world around them. Because visual management can do this, we find that visual management workplaces that have been well designed for the tasks they are supposed to achieve can outperform more traditional workplaces.

We have all heard the phrase "a picture is worth a thousand words." Time and again, history has proven the wisdom of this expression. Visual images are what typically come to mind when we think about key events in recent history. Although millions of words have been written about the United States in Vietnam, for example, what we remember are the images of soldiers, prisoners, and children rather than the words. The same is true of major natural disasters, such as California's Loma Prieta earthquake in October 1989, the reality of which was captured forever in our minds in the images of a collapsing freeway, one of which is shown in Figure 2-3. In the same way that photographs and video today provide visual cues to the essence of events, in previous centuries great works of art provided powerful images that conveyed great amounts of information. Yet, despite the power of visual images, society has traditionally relied on the written word to convey more detailed information.

This reliance on the written word has persisted in our organizations despite significant advances in other forms of communication. When there was no television, everyone who had an education read. With the introduction of movies, television, computers, and other visual media, however, people have come to rely less and less on the written word for information. We spend more time watching television and motion pictures and less time reading. We have become a society of watchers instead of a society of readers. But our companies still expect us, as employees, to read everything that is important to our work. They have virtually ignored our transition from immersion

Figure 2-3. The visual message in this photo of the Cypress Viaduct in Oakland, California, after the 1989 Loma Prieta earthquake carries home the destructiveness of a powerful earthquake in ways no words can convey. (Photograph by H. G. Wilshire, U.S. Geological Survey.)

in the written word to captivation by images, and they have done little to transform their own communication systems to meet changing employee expectations. The result has been information overload and tuned-out employees.

Inconsistencies Among Communication Elements

Another issue that organizations must address is the lack of consistency and alignment among the communication elements. Everything that one can see in an organization sends a message, even a blank wall. Yet most organizations have not thought about the messages they are sending or about the potential impact of some of their inadvertent messages.

The next time you enter a retail establishment such as a bookstore, look around and see what messages are being sent to you, the customer. Do you find a comfortable chair in which you can sit and peruse a volume or two? Are the aisles wide enough for easy browsing, and is there enough light to see the books? Are the colors on the walls and in the carpet coordinated and pleasant? Is soft background music playing? Are there point-of-purchase displays that encourage impulse buying? Typically, these messages are ones of welcome, ones that encourage browsing, and ones that encourage you to purchase.

What would you see if you could enter the employee area of the same bookstore, though? Many employee areas sport bare walls and concrete floors; the furniture tends to be utilitarian, mismatched, and uncomfortable; and the space is often crowded and dark. There are places for employees to keep their personal belongings, but there is little to show that this is an important part of the company, and little to keep employees focused on what is important in their work. A clear message is sent here, also, although it may have unintended consequences. Employees often believe that they are being told that they should not spend time in their space, even on breaks; that their break space is unimportant to the company; and that they are much less valuable than the customer. The stark contrast between the public space and the employee space shows a lack of synergy between these elements and can have a negative impact on employee behavior.

In addition, and more important, the organization is missing a tremendous opportunity to manage its visual communication in a way that helps the employees focus on its mission and performance expectations. What if employee spaces were clean and uncluttered and had well-designed displays of key performance indicators that were updated frequently enough to hold the employees' attention? What if some of these displays reminded the employees of their own importance and the importance of their customers? How would employees feel if they were treated as well as the customers in such an establishment? What message would that send? How could the organization reduce the inconsistencies in design and communication that reinforce the wrong messages?

As in a fine painting, there is a multilayered complexity in the design of a visual management workplace. What we see is the sum of many parts. An artist, for example, begins with an image in her mind; this is equivalent to the mission and vision of the organization. She then sketches the structure and broad outline of the image onto canvas. She spends a great deal of time on the drawing because this is the foundation for the work of art she is trying to create; this is equivalent to the initial design phase in our organizations. From there, she adds a broad color scheme and identifies the points of strongest lights and darks. These points of contrast are crucial to the finished piece: The entire painting must hold together in a coherent fashion or it will fail to achieve the artist's vision. The artist continues in this manner, adding detail and accents and ensuring that all parts are working in harmony, until the work is completed. The artist has used all of her talent, skills, and resources to achieve her vision, just as organizations will do in implementing visual management.

Imagine for a moment that an organization has aligned all of its visual elements in the same way that a great artist does, so that what you see is coherent, connected, and focused. All elements are focused on the central mission and vision of the organization, just as they are focused on a central image in great art.

In Vermeer's masterpiece *An Artist in His Studio*, shown in Figure 2-4, we see clearly what happens when all of the key elements (drawing, design, light, tone, perspective, shape, and even brush strokes) work together so well that the finished work is much greater than the sum of those individual elements. This is exactly what we want to do in an organizational setting. We want to integrate all of the organizational and fine arts design elements into a structure and a set of outcomes that is more effective than any independent or uncoordinated single structure or outcome could be.

Imagine that this central focus, or alignment, allows people to feel, see, and touch the mission, vision, and core values of the organization, as well as its culture and its goals. Imagine, too, that the visual elements provide employees with an unprecedented amount of immediate, understandable information that enables them to focus clearly on solving systemic problems and improving organizational out-

Figure 2-4. Vermeer's masterpiece, An Artist in His Studio, *is the fine arts equivalent of what visual management attempts to achieve in organizations: All of the key elements work together to produce an outcome that is much greater than the sum of its parts.* (Photograph courtesy of the Kunsthistorisches Museum, Vienna, Austria.)

comes. And imagine that the aligned visual elements give everyone who sees them a sense of belonging and of being important to the organization. This is the goal of visual management in any organization: to reinforce system alignment and improve the organization's performance. Visual management is all about working better, not about looking good, although looking good is a great side benefit.

_____ ■ _____

CHAPTER 3

Foundations for Visual Management

Visual management is a system that helps organizations create and sustain a competitive advantage in two significant ways. First, it ensures that an organization's internal structure, management systems, work environment, and culture are aligned with its mission and values. Second, it focuses employees' attention on critical performance goals, making sure that the employees know what is expected of them at all times and are committed to the organization's success. It is a holistic and systemic approach to the improvement of individual and organizational performance. Visual management works in any well-designed organization that is committed to aligning its operating systems and processes with its mission and goals, and it can be used to strengthen and support this alignment in organizations that are engaged in the design or redesign process.

Visual management is, in many ways, a natural response to the escalating pace of work that has been created by the proliferation of information, as discussed in Chapter 2; to increasing demands for better and faster performance; and to the need to make sense of this in a rapidly changing social context. Today's business-oriented newspapers, magazines, journals, and books repeatedly tell us that organizations feel pressure to perform exceedingly well in an increasingly complex and dynamic business environment. They also report that aligning systems, strategies, people, and competencies is crucial to achieving this exceptional performance. In the wake of such prolific advice, all manner of design and improvement plans, processes, and paradigms have been created to address these issues. We often find, though, that the range of choices is so wide and so varied that even trying to decide which choice to make can divert attention from some core activities that are crucial to success.

Today's most effective organizations, however, are designed to ensure that technical, structural, decision-making, information, reward, and human resource systems are synchronized to best meet and serve their goals and needs. They seek connections among the work that needs to be accomplished, the people who must do the work, and the customers who use their output, and they have parlayed the alignment of people, processes, and systems into top performance. Yet, even in the best of these organizations, managers struggle to improve results and to lead and motivate employees who often feel disconnected from their work and from the organization of which they are a part. These are the areas that are directly addressed by visual management systems.

In this chapter, we highlight the factors, disciplines, and practices that have helped build the foundation for visual management, and show how the power of the visual management system is rooted in the careful interweaving of great organization design, a clearly defined mission and vision, sound human resource management, and fine arts principles. First, let's look at where visual management comes from.

■ Where Does Visual Management Come From?

The concept of visual management did not spring fully developed from any one discipline or stream of work in organizational change and improvement. It has grown incrementally and has evolved concurrently with the increasing emphasis that current management practice places on people and systems alignment, performance improvement, and customer focus. It addresses the growing challenge of information overload, as well as the burning need to share the right information with employees and other important constituents, and it is helping to drive the growing trend in many fields to make information visual. Further, and uniquely, it ties all of these concepts together using fine arts principles.

In essence, visual management is a system that has been developed on a foundation of proven management practice buttressed by fine arts. It is grounded in the strategic focus of the organization, and its growth and development have been driven most directly by the needs of visionary leaders who are seeking new ways to improve organizational performance and by their ongoing concern with cultural change as a way to improve performance.

Strategic Focus

From the early thinking about strategy in organizations to more recent concerns with building competitive advantage and developing learning organizations, leaders and managers have continued to focus their attention and resources on developing and clarifying why their organizations exist and what they are in business to do. No matter what the language used to describe and explain the latest strategic model or theory may be, good leaders understand that the best and most effective organizations have a clear strategic focus and have aligned their operating systems to best meet the goals of their strategies and the needs of their customers.

For example, a broad spectrum of business and service organizations has adopted supply-chain analysis and planning as a means of refining the coordination of internal processes and reframing alignment among internal work units. The supply chain typically links the overall functions of a business, looking at the flow of materials, products, and/or services across the procurement, transformation, and distribution functions within the organization. Supply-chain concepts lead naturally into the value-chain concepts that seem so important to current strategic thinking; value chains link internal and external constituencies based on the value added at each critical step of the process. The value-chain model serves to highlight the need for functional alignment of operating systems to meet customer demands. Most business models utilized today are based to a great degree on the importance of customer focus, and most mission and vision statements indicate that the organization is striving for improved customer focus. The customer has become central to the strategies and operating principles of today's organizations and their leaders.

Leadership

Leadership is one of the most rapidly expanding areas of inquiry in organizational research today. Look at the bookshelves in any business library or in the business section of a large bookstore and you will find a wide selection of titles and topics from which to choose. Some leadership books sing the praises of individual leaders, others look at leadership as a system in organizations, and still others question the how and why of effective leadership. Despite the different questions being raised in such studies, we find some common ground among them that has informed the work of visual management.

In most organizations, improved leadership is believed to be an important contributor to meeting the performance improvement challenge. In fact, it is unusual to find an organization that does not relate the quality of leadership to performance in some way. What is interesting, though, is that many of the stories we hear or read about the leadership-performance link are negative ones. We are told what is wrong with leadership in a given area and why performance suffers as a result. Supervisors, for example, are notoriously blamed for the failure of change programs in their organizations, despite the fact that they are left out of planning for change efforts as often today as they were twenty years ago when they were first being replaced by teams. Entry-level managers are often selected from among the ranks of the hourly workers because they are excellent at the work they are doing;

they are put into these leadership positions without adequate training or support to help them succeed, and we are told that the unit's failure to improve is the result of poor leadership.

Studies of leadership, in general, suggest that certain personal attributes are important to effective leadership: honesty, commitment, a willingness to change and to deal with uncertainty, and an unerring ability to motivate or even inspire people. We also hear that strong leadership requires strategic thinking and global awareness along with a clear vision and direction. There is little question, though, about organizations' need for and reliance on strong, solid leadership to achieve their goals.

Over the long run, organizations are ultimately only as good as are their leaders and their leadership systems. The press champions a group of leaders in a variety of business settings for their business acumen and even for their personal charisma. Look at the leaders of some well-known U.S. technology companies, such as Jeff Bezos (Amazon.com), Carly Fiorina (Hewlett-Packard), Bill Gates (Microsoft), or Meg Whitman (eBay). All of them share the ability to focus on a clear and compelling vision and the capacity to engage their organization in following that vision. In other sectors, leaders like Jack Welch (GE) turned their attention unceasingly to performance and either improved or cut nonperforming businesses and people. In each instance, the organization was strengthened and its performance improved as a result of the vision, passion, and commitment of such a leader.

We believe, as much of the leadership research tells us, that outcomes are directly related to the quality of leadership, both that of individual leaders and that of the leadership systems that are developed. These lessons have been integrated into the visual management process, both through insistence on top leadership support and by integrating leaders at all levels into the development and implementation of visual management. In this way, visual management helps leaders use visual systems as a strategic approach to performance improvement.

Culture

Some popular management practices and paradigms today focus on the people in the organization and highlight the importance of the culture and people systems that an organization creates in order to meet its goals. Culture means many things to many people, but in organizational terms, it typically refers to the work ethic, the expectations for behavior, and the collective attitudes, assumptions, and basic beliefs that are shared by people in the organization.[1] Culture is influenced by a host of variables, including leadership, reporting relationships and structure, work design, and the surrounding social fabric. In turn, culture directly influences patterns of behavior and their outcomes.

The business literature and the popular press are rife with stories of organizations that are attempting to build cultures that are consistent with what they want to achieve or to change their cultures in order to influence their outcomes. Think about the tales of Harley-Davidson's comeback, in which a culture of poor workmanship and antagonistic customer relations was transformed into a culture in which employees learned to value high quality and fought to regain and maintain customer loyalty. Or reflect back to the mid-1990s, when Marriott found it increasingly difficult to recruit the kind of people it needed, despite its reputation for excellent customer service, and initiated a significant change program to improve the culture so that it could attract appropriate talent. Look at the cultures that have been created and sustained by companies such as Southwest Airlines. In all these cases, we see organizations that have realized that culture is a critical resource that can have an enormous impact on performance and results.

Organizational culture has become a primary target of most change programs today, and conventional wisdom suggests that to bring about lasting change in an organization, the culture must be adjusted to support the newly desired environment. To us, this means that an organization that is interested in improving its performance in terms of better customer service, higher quality, and a stronger return for the organization, for example, must invest in and sustain a culture in which people care about these results. It must also support a culture in which people feel important and respected.

Human Resource Systems

We know from decades of study that organizations that pay appropriate attention to the people working for them reap benefits in terms of performance outcomes. Motivated and committed employees work harder and achieve better results. And the best results are achieved from people who know what is expected of them and who have the skills and capacity to deliver those results.

Much of the research tells us, too, that the development of appropriate human resource systems will have a dramatic impact on organizational performance. Hiring and selection systems that match skills and potential to job requirements ensure that individuals who cannot perform adequately will not be hired. Placement and internal selection processes that ensure that employees understand their jobs and know their potential for advancement reinforce the importance of employees to the organization. Reward and recognition systems that support fair and equitable pay plans and that link rewards to performance emphasize the idea that pay for performance is important to the organization. Training and education systems that target the right lessons and encourage learning and improvement keep people alert and ensure that skill development is an ongoing process. Perhaps most important, performance measurement and reporting systems that provide direct, fair, and consistent performance feedback contribute significantly to effective individual performance.

Visual management has drawn from each of these lessons, and it supports human resource systems in several ways. Because of its emphasis on performance at all levels, it ensures that people know their own performance levels relative to those of the rest of their team, group, or unit. The results reported by visual management systems are often used to identify employees' training or educational needs, and recommendations for training typically come as no surprise in organizations that have adopted visual management. Visual management also reports results in financial terms, including shared bonus and reward payouts, so that people can see the direct link between pay and performance. Overall, visual management has utilized the findings from much of this body of research to support its performance improvement focus.

Management Practice and Visual Management

Current management practice focuses attention on improving the internal workings of organizations in order to enhance their performance. It deals with the development of strategic initiatives and focus in organizations; it emphasizes the importance of mission, vision, and guiding values as creators and sustainers of organizational cultures; it directs our attention to the impact of good leadership and followership on organizational performance; and it emphasizes the importance of sound human resource practices in effective organizations. In fact, current management thought and practice focus clearly on many of the building blocks that provide the foundation for visual management.

Some schools of thought concerning ways to improve organizational performance concentrate on developing appropriate strategies to compete in particular markets. Some focus on building internal cultures that are capable of supporting individual and group performance improvement. Some focus on structural variables, such as reporting relationships, work teams, and organizational frameworks. Others focus on the impact of leadership on outcomes. All, however, have a common goal: the improvement of the organization and its performance across the board.

An organization that supports a particular strategic mission and culture requires leaders who can engage people effectively in the ongoing pursuit of that mission and the sustenance of that culture. Over the years, we have been privileged to know and work with some leaders who recognized that using visuals for performance feedback could reinforce a culture of performance, and that relying on visual mechanisms for more effective communication could also create an interesting and energetic setting for the work. Some posted cost and output data at work stations, others tried to improve the look and flow of the physical space in order to improve work processes, and still others created displays about customers and employees to reinforce the importance of both groups to the organization. These managers' efforts acknowledged the power of visuals, but the managers did not yet see the power of an integrated approach that meshed the visuals carefully with their strategies, mission, and operating systems.

■ System Design and Visual Management

As we will state several times in this book, visual management will not reach its full potential unless it is implemented in a well-designed organization, or unless sound organization design is an explicit part of the implementation process. This design is critical to the alignment of the management systems that are supported by visual management.

At the core of organization design practice is an effort to align major organizational systems in such a way as to best achieve the mission of the unit. In other words, we want to arrange the major components of the organization so as to ensure that the throughput, or conversion process, guarantees the outcomes that we desire. Yet, organizations do not operate in a vacuum: They are affected by external environmental forces, such as markets and governments as well as by internal factors and characteristics. Organizations, then, are open systems that manage their contexts with a clearly defined purpose and mission, carefully designed operating systems, and effective mechanisms for feedback. Figure 3-1 shows a simplified diagrammatic overview of the organization as an open system and tells us that inputs from the environment, combined with the factors of production, are transformed through some organized conversion processes into desired outputs in the form of products or services. The conversion process is designed from among a range of choices concerning what

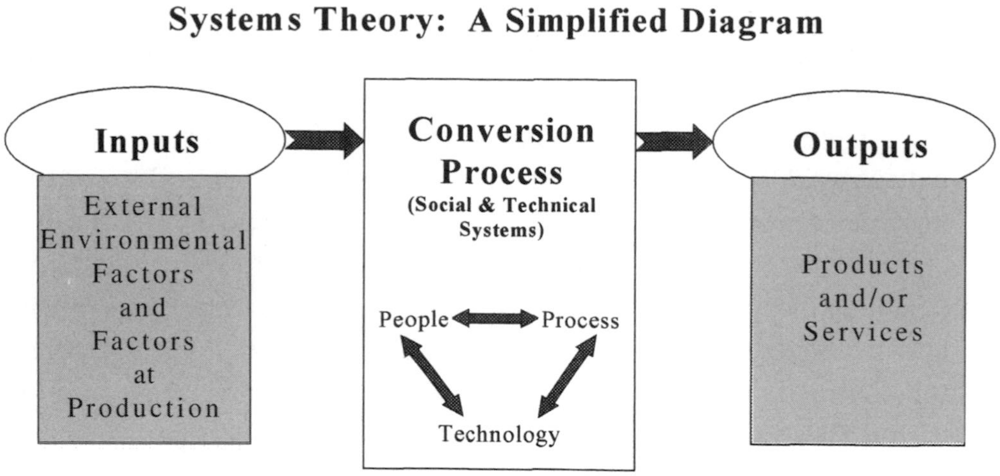

Systems Theory: A Simplified Diagram

```
┌─────────────────┐      ┌──────────────────┐      ┌─────────────────┐
│    Inputs       │ ──▶  │   Conversion     │ ──▶  │    Outputs      │
│                 │      │     Process      │      │                 │
│   External      │      │ (Social & Technical │     │                 │
│  Environmental  │      │    Systems)      │      │    Products     │
│   Factors       │      │                  │      │    and/or        │
│     and         │      │  People ◀──▶ Process │     │    Services     │
│   Factors       │      │       ↘    ↙      │      │                 │
│     at          │      │    Technology    │      │                 │
│  Production     │      │                  │      │                 │
└─────────────────┘      └──────────────────┘      └─────────────────┘
```

Figure 3-1. An organization is an open system that uses purpose and mission to manage its context, frame its operating systems, and ensure effective feedback for improvement.

the organization wants to be and the types of systems it will use to become that entity.

Conversion processes are composed of both human (social) and production (technical) systems, and the best conversion processes are those that jointly optimize these two systems within the organization. This means that the organization does not create a system based primarily on the technological imperative simply because the technology exists, nor does it create a system solely for the good of the people in it. Rather, organizational processes are developed that intentionally balance the demands on and the capacities of people and technology, and that optimize the relationship between the two to best meet the demands of the organization and achieve its desired outputs. This emphasis on the social and technical systems does not come about by happenstance. Sociotechnical systems theory tells us clearly that the best-performing organizations have done a remarkable job of balancing the interaction between the social and technical systems so that they work in concert to deliver the desired end product or service,[2] and this is an important concept in effective organization design.

Organization Design

Organization design has contributed in significant ways to the development of visual management. The turbulence of today's business and economic environment forces organizations to constantly reassess their competitive positions and, often, to reconfigure their structures and operating systems to better meet the new challenges they face. Unfortunately, all too often, organizations have undertaken major change and improvement projects in response to these rapidly changing external environments without first determining whether they have the internal capacity to achieve their desired ends. Without an appropriate structure or consistent operating systems, these organizations often set themselves up for failure in both the change project undertaken and the achievement of the desired results.

Organization design brings to the table a set of principles and activities that can help organizations determine the best structures and systems for achieving their stated mission. There are many choices of organization design approaches and methods, all of which have several characteristics and goals in common. Traditional sociotechnical systems analysis and design is a detailed, methodical, and carefully documented approach to designing systems and structures, for example. Accelerated design methodologies, often based on sociotechnical system principles, have become popular in the face of rapid changes in competitive environments and conditions. Participative design is another powerful and clearly defined design process that helps in the definition of structure and appropriate systems in changing organizations.[3] All of these rely on group and individual input into a process that is intended to create a framework of people, processes, technology, and systems that will carry the organization forward to new levels of success. All require strong and devoted leadership. And all have met with varied success.

The failures, though, do not usually result from the choice of methodology. More often, they result from an inappropriate rationale for the change to begin with, inattention to necessary detail during planning and implementation, or a lack of support or follow-up within the organization during the transition process. Sometimes these processes flounder because the organization assumed that change would be achieved by a knight in shining armor who rode to the rescue; sometimes the organization assumed that the change process was owned by a design team and no other input was needed; and sometimes people across the organization did not understand the need for change, were not adequately prepared for its personal impact on them, or were not involved in the process. One of the key lessons we take from a review of organization design methodologies and practices is that involvement is important to the ultimate success of the project. We also know that there is a range of good choices of methods to use to design the systems, but the methods must fit the capabilities and character of the organization. As Richard Axelrod makes clear in his book *Terms of Engagement*, it is the principles behind the process that make a difference in the long run.[4]

To review the design of an organization, we often use our own variation of a model developed by our colleague, Paul Gustavson, which he calls the Organizational Systems Design (OSD) Model.[5] As you can see in Figure 3-2, the organizational conversion process in this model is shown as a set of choices that the organization must consider. These choices influence the behaviors, feelings, and attributes of the people in the organization, which in turn influence the outcomes. The choices are of two types: The first set is about defining the organization's mission, vision, guiding principles, strategies, and goals; and the second set is about the systems that will be developed to carry out the mission. Behaviors, feelings, and attributes are viewed as resulting from the choices made.

In visual management, we focus heavily on these two sets of choices. They form two of the three dimensions of the performance improvement process, and they serve as the foundation for the visual overlay that is the third dimension. As you will see more clearly in Chapters 5 and 6, we work hard in visual management implementations to define, refine, and align the choices made concerning the

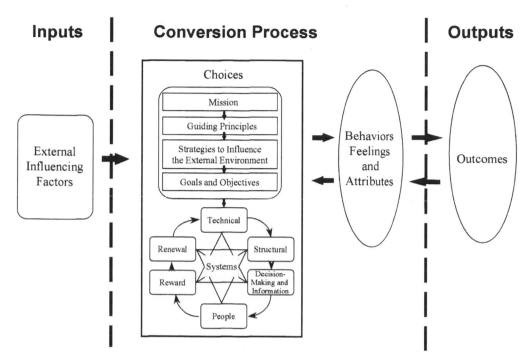

Figure 3-2. Using a comprehensive model like the Organizational Systems Design Model to develop or assess design elements is crucial to understanding the choices an organization makes about its mission and the systems it will use to achieve that mission.

mission and vision of the organization. These must align with the organization's core purpose, and the strategies developed to accomplish the mission and the specific goals of these strategies must also be in alignment. If they are not, there is a great danger of creating well-designed visual systems that reinforce the wrong things. Similarly, we typically look at people and reward systems together, although they are separate in this model.

Once we are clear about the mission, then it is important to ensure that the actual organizational operating systems, the core systems that make the organization what it is, are designed to align directly with the mission. Technical systems include procedures, technology, and the physical plant. Within these systems, we work to ensure that the work flow makes sense given the organization's mission and goals, that operating policies and procedures support the mission, and that the technology is appropriate for the organization's purpose. The structural system refers to the actual organization structure, and it is important to ensure that the reporting relationships make sense given the purpose and mission of the organization. The decision-making and information systems include those elements that are designed to develop and manage data, methods and mechanisms for organizationwide communication, and the authority and responsibility structure in the organization. The people systems are the human resource functions, including selection, training, appraisal, reward, recognition, and retention procedures and policies. Renewal systems include the planning and review processes that provide feedback for organizational learning.

Keep in mind that none of these systems is a stand-alone element; there is much interaction and overlap among them. Although the OSD model appears to treat each of these areas as separate and distinct, we typically look at them in concert, and we often collapse them into three or four critical areas. For example, we typically look at structure and decision making as a single complex operating system, and do not separate the two parts as we review or redesign this system. The important idea to remember, however, is that choices must be made, and that we need useful models that can help us identify the range of systems choices we should consider so that we can best align the systems to the organization's purpose and mission. Systems are designed for particular types of outcomes, and if they are not in alignment, we may inadvertently produce outcomes that we do not desire.

Roots of Organizational Excellence Are in the Design

There is an adage among organization designers that says that each organization is perfectly designed to achieve the results it actually gets. The problem with this, of course, is that some organizations have not been deliberately designed to achieve their actual results, and this poses a significant challenge. If results occur by happenstance, there is no methodical and predictable way to influence those results in a particular direction. Organization design, in the best of circumstances, is a deliberate activity that creates a structure, a set of reporting relationships, work guidelines, and the other supporting structures and systems that make up the actual framework of the organization. Sound organization design practice means designing to meet a specific mission that has been carefully crafted by the organization. Effective design brings all of the elements of an organization—its people, processes, and systems—into an appropriately aligned state so that the interaction of these variables can deliver the desired outcomes identified by the mission.

Performance, Information, and Visual Literacy

We have heard managers in many companies talk about the need to boost performance at the individual, group, and organizational levels. Some of them have produced dozens of reports and documents and have held large meetings during which they projected images of complex financial statements on large screens, all intended to tell people how their units and the organization were doing. These managers summarized their information on sales, inventories, throughput, employment, compensation, distribution, training, and planning and sent it out in memos, e-mails, and other written formats to employees who were asking for more and better information. The managers, who were trying to meet these employee demands openly and honestly, seemed to believe that if the information were made available in full written form, employees would be able to absorb it and use it to change and improve their performance. Unfortunately, many of these managers had missed an important factor of organizational life: Information overload, particularly the explosion of written information, is blinding people to most of the data available and is blocking their ability to absorb even the most basic, yet important, information related to their own work and the work of the unit or organization.

We realized that in order to cut through the information overload and help people see clearly what they must do if they are to achieve the goals of their organization, we needed to develop mechanisms that got the right information to the right people in the right ways. This meant first ensuring that the design of the organization had created internal strategic and structural alignment with its mission, and then appealing directly to the ways in which people took in information and learned to use it, in order to keep them focused on the desired outcomes. And that meant doing something other than simply providing written documentation and hoping for improvement. In other words, we had to find a way to help organizations ensure that the information that people needed in order to perform well was information that they knew they needed. And we had to help organizations understand that this information had to be available when the people needed it and in a form that could be easily understood and internalized. To us, this meant that organizations had to do a better job of managing employee performance and employee expectations by *deliberately managing what people see*.

A Trend Toward Making Things Visual

There has been growing interest in the concept of visual workplaces in the manufacturing sector of our economy, particularly as the emphasis on lean production systems has spread in the last decade. The Japanese 5-S process, which is often incorporated into lean production systems, is a model that relies to a great extent on the notion of a visual workplace in order to help organize a production operation. Yet the visual workplace in 5-S is to our concept of visual management as cleaning an existing house is to designing, building, and maintaining a new one. In other words, the 5-S process is a cleanup and sorting process that creates a clean and uncluttered workspace, but it does not address directly the design or alignment activities that are central to visual management.

In fact, the five *S*s are *seiri* (sorting), *seiton* (arranging), *seiso* (cleaning), *seiketsu* (standardizing or integrating the first three into the work), and *shitsuke* (consistency or discipline of follow-through). This set of activities brings visual order to a workplace, ensuring that it is clean, safe, predictable, and arranged in such a way that excess motion and energy need not be expended to accomplish the task at hand. The visual concepts of 5-S and the visual systems referred to in much that is written about visual workplaces[6] are not bad concepts; they simply are limited in focus and are not designed to deliver the far-reaching impact of the visual management systems we are describing in this book. The visual systems in the 5-S environment focus on clean, organized, and safe workplaces and the actions necessary to create them; the visual systems in a visual management environment specifically refer to the broader range of management tools and systems created by visual management practice that permeate the organization.

Once they have been introduced to the concepts of such a visual management system, leaders and managers begin to see that it has a depth, a substance, and an applicability far beyond that intended by 5-S, a depth and substance that can sustain the visual management process and its results over the long term. They learn that the visual management process has been carefully designed to improve performance across the entire organization, utilizing a broad range of visual enhancements to keep people focused on the organization's mission, desired outcomes, and appropriate goals; and they find that its adopters develop a good working knowledge of the key organizational elements and systems that need to be aligned in order to improve performance. So, in order to help newcomers to visual management see the power of the process, it is important to help them understand clearly and fully the foundation upon which a good visual management process rests.

As we have already shown, people are becoming more and more visual. Technological advances reinforce the visual nature of information sharing and communication and continue to increase our reliance on visual cues for gathering information. What the fine arts give us is a means of making these visual cues interesting, exciting, and memorable. We already know that visual management intends to put critical information in front of employees and other stakeholders in ways that cannot be ignored. We also know that we want workers to have performance data constantly available in such a manner that they are attuned to this information and use it to guide their behavior. If we incorporate the principles of design, color, and shape from the fine arts disciplines when we create our visual messages, then we are creating them from strength and consistency rather than in a haphazard manner.

Visual Literacy

One of the reasons that visual enhancements can work so well in visual management organizations is that society in general is increasingly coming to rely on visual messages to gather information, and visual literacy is on the rise. Visual literacy refers to a person's ability to learn from visual messages, first through decoding and then through interpretation. What any person "sees" is really a combination of vision and thought: The images seen through the eyes are interpreted through the lens of experience and knowledge. Consider the symbols depicted in Figure 3-3. The first, a circle with a diagonal line through it, tells us not to do something. The second, a circle with a question mark in its center, is used to identify a location where we can get information or answers to our questions. The third, an arrow, tells us which direction to go in. But how would we know what these meant if we did not combine our vision with thought or experience to decipher them? Or think, for example, about those yellow triangular signs posted throughout most organizations. Most people know that they are warning signs of some type. We see the shape and color, and even if we don't step up and read them, we know that they are warning signs because we interpret them based on something we have already learned.

Visual literacy is a key phenomenon that we hook into with visual management. We teach people what they need to know in order to perform well and to understand what it takes to do this, and we create visual messages that capture and enhance what people have already learned so that they can respond appropriately to what the message says. Visual messages condense the content so that it can be quickly

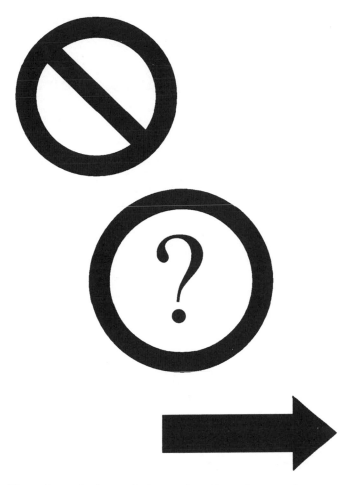

Figure 3-3. Visual symbols and signs give clear instructions, even when we cannot speak the language of the area in which they are posted.

interpreted using both sight and thought capacities that are mutually reinforcing. We construct the visual media in such a way that they capture people's attention; we train people to know where and when to look for specific types of messages; and we constantly reinforce these lessons until we know that they have been internalized. In this way, visual management both reinforces visual literacy and relies on that literacy for part of its success. Therefore, the careful and thoughtful construction of a visual management environment must take into account the impact of visual messages on the people in these systems, and the visual messages that are sent in this environment should be crafted with great care to ensure that the message that is sent is the one that is received.

■ Fine Arts and Visual Management

The fine arts add a critical and vital dimension to the practice of visual management and to the development of effective visual messages that have a systematic, deliberate, and coordinated focus that emphasizes what is important to the organization and its many constituents. The principles of design in the fine arts help us focus our attention on how best to present the information that is required in order to spur the performance improvements that are central to visual management.

In art, design (or composition) is the arrangement of elements within the format of the work. We think of these elements in terms of lines, light and shade, color, and mass. The composition of a picture, for example, might start in the center of a light area, then proceed along the edge of a significant shape, move to the middle of a dark object, and then end with a bright color accent. While each element may initially appear independent, the key is to think of all of them in an integrated fashion within the design of that picture. Each element is capable of carrying the design and of making or breaking it. When we think about using these elements in a visual management project, they guide our choices about the physical changes we will make to a facility.

Without becoming too detailed, let's look at the impact of some of these design elements in order to better understand how and why we might utilize them in the visual management environment. A strong horizontal emphasis in a work of art generally implies calm, restfulness, and peace. We might, for example, establish a strong horizontal line of photos and other memorabilia in a lobby or break area to help the people there relax. Or we might design horizontal planes directly into a room or building to enhance the message of restfulness and peace, much as Columbus Regional Hospital (CRH) has done in its new patient rooms, as shown in Figure 3-4.

Figure 3-4. The horizontal lines of patient rooms at Columbus Regional Hospital reinforce a feeling of peace, calm, and restfulness.

Diagonals usually imply action or motion. Think about the earnings or performance charts we often see in business review meetings: Upward diagonals hint at good forward movement, and downward diagonals often signal negative movement or performance. The shape of these charts sends these messages whether or not we can see what each axis actually represents. Jagged shapes usually imply pain and tension, and we often feel this when we look at the ups and downs of charts showing stock performance. For example, look at Figure 3-5. However, a pyramid usually implies stability or permanence, while rounded shapes imply rest and have soothing connotations. A V shape can imply insecurity, and a circle suggests perfection. Careful use of these principles of line and shape can enhance the visual messages we send in our organizations. A deliberate and structured plan for using such design principles in the visual plan strengthens the entire

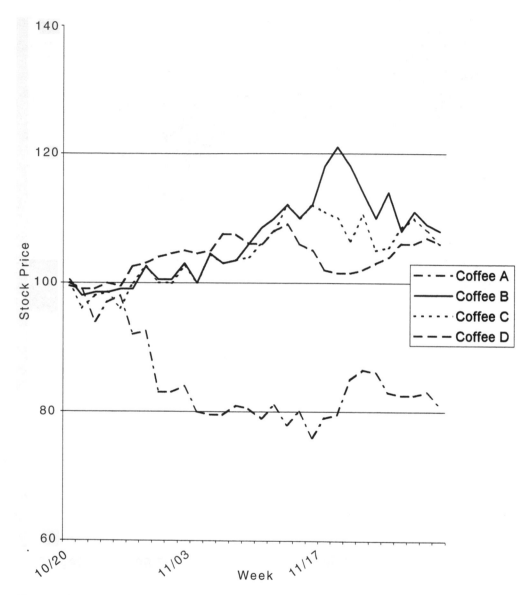

Figure 3-5. Volatile stock price performance charts are depicted with jagged lines. They typically reflect tension. Or is this a caffeine buzz?

process and improves the physical manifestation of visual management.

In the same way that we use these design principles in developing the visual plan, we use the fine arts concepts of contrast, consonance, and color to help us plan the overall impact of the visuals. Contrast adds emphasis within or among the visuals and the displays. Consonance refers to the unity of the design, and paying attention to consonance helps guard against the disconnected feel of randomly selected or carelessly arranged visuals. Color, of course, can have universal overtones of emotion. Red typically means fire and danger and hence grabs attention quickly. Yellow connotes warmth and joy and is also a color that people gravitate toward. Blue can symbolize peace, quiet, and/or cold, depending upon the shade chosen and the intensity of the hue. Green is the color of plants and can represent freshness or restfulness. Black usually represents fear and death; its boldness can be softened by sparing use or the use of other colors.

In addition to drawing upon the emotional impact of colors, we may use them in a variety of combinations to spark a series of different effects, and our selection and use of color is important to the visual management environment. This lesson may seem ironic since this book has been produced in black and white. Yet the contrast among various colors can be imagined from many of the photos in the figures, and color is a fine arts concept that most of us have some familiarity with already.

■ Visual Management: A Three-Dimensional Approach

Organization design brings the concept of organizational systems alignment to visual management. As we saw in the discussion of organizational systems design, the management systems must be synchronized if they are to best support the most effective and powerful performance in organizations. If those systems do not work in concert, the resulting imbalance can lead to unanticipated and inappropriate performance results.

Its mission, vision, guiding values, strategies, and goals define what the organization wants to be; the human, technical, and support systems create operating structures that define how the organization will achieve its mission. The interaction among these components results in behavior that drives particular outcomes. If an organization pays attention to only these two components (the design of the organization and its mission), it has a running start on defining itself and identifying a preferred path for performance. Yet, it has not ensured that its people will understand what it wants or what they need to do to achieve this. In other words, it has developed an aligned system, but it has not created effective mechanisms to enable employees to see and understand their importance and how they affect the desired processes and outcomes. A third component is needed to ensure that this happens.

Visual management enhances these two core dimensions of good organization design by combining them with a third critical dimension; it makes system alignment a three-dimensional process through the added use of visual enhancements. Think about it this way: Can words alone capture the power of raising the American flag at Iwo Jima, or the utter devastation at the sinking of the *USS Arizona* at Pearl Harbor, as seen in Figure 3-6? Could words alone have communicated the tragedy of September 11? Or is the real story and power in the visual images? Have you ever participated in a factory tour that left you excited and energized in some way that you had not anticipated? If you are ever in Waterbury, Vermont, visit Ben & Jerry's for a fascinating factory tour, filled with visual information, humor, color, and a spirit of fun and hard work. Organizations like this are fun and inspiring to visit, and this is part of what visual management can do for its users. But please keep in mind that what you see is only part of the total story. Visual management does not simply make a workplace into a fun tour center or a museum; it creates a living work of art that focuses attention on critical performance requirements and results in such a way that it inspires better performance.

The three-dimensional approach that allows us to do this combines a clearly defined organizational mission and vision with excel-

Figure 3-6. Words alone cannot capture the sense of loss, anger, and devastation felt by Americans when the USS Arizona *was sunk at Pearl Harbor.* (Photograph courtesy of The Franklin D. Roosevelt Library Digital Archives.)

lent organization design and careful integration with visual elements. In organizational terms, the addition of visuals as the third design dimension makes all the difference here: It creates an environment in which the systems affect people on a deeper and more profound level, enhancing their ability to deliver what is needed in a more committed and effective manner. At the same time, it simplifies the complexities of design by making the design choices clear and visible.

CHAPTER 4

Visual Management in Action

The visual management organization is designed to be, first and foremost, a top-performing organization. A focus on mission and vision, attention to quality leadership, reliance on employee expertise, training to enhance performance, solid and continuous performance feedback, exemplary customer service, and the linkage of these activities to rewards and recognition are some of the basic activities of any top-performing organization. They are also required for the top-performing visual management organization. The core difference is that the visual management organization addresses these issues visually. It has codified its mission, vision, values, and goals into a road map or some other graphic that shows all of its employees, customers, and other stakeholders where it intends to go and how it intends to get there. This visual road map or graphic serves a centralizing and focal purpose, and reinforces for each and every employee his purpose in the organization.

The organization has arranged its physical space in such a way as to promote efficiency and effectiveness, reorganizing work areas into coherent units that include the relevant tools and information necessary to complete the tasks. It has created a war room,[1] a central space in which performance data are clearly and boldly displayed so that employees know and understand how they and their teams are doing at any given point in time. The visual management organization has dedicated space to displays of company history, the organization's mission and goals, employee achievements, and customer desires and feedback. Most important, it has filled all its workplace with visual images that demand a focus on the organization's mission, goals, and performance.

■ Stories from the Field

The visual management organization is unique in the way in which it incorporates visual literacy into its working environment to ensure that people and processes work together to improve performance. It has created a space in which no employee can mistake the mission, her reason for being in the organization, or what is required of her, and it is this visual environment that reinforces the performance requirements and the organization's vision for its people. This visual environment permeates the organization, serving as a coordination and integration vehicle. Some examples of real visual management organizations will show what we mean by all of this.

ZiLOG

ZiLOG, Inc., is a semiconductor company based in San Jose, California, the heart of Silicon Valley. ZiLOG's products include microprocessors, microcontrollers, and digital signal processors used in consumer electronics and appliances, factory automation, building control, financial transaction processing, and the automotive aftermarket. The company reports that it is the top worldwide supplier of controllers for universal infrared remote controls.[2] ZiLOG relies on its technological expertise, time-to-market consciousness, and integrated solutions for customers to guarantee its market success. This requires tremendous capability, creativity, and flexibility on the part of its employees.

ZiLOG has used visual management to support its strategy, to foster creativity among employees, and to enhance communication. The ZiLOG employee communications board, part of which is shown in Figure 4-1, features a series of drawings that literally show the employees where the company is going. Four graphic panels represent the organization's mission, history, and goals; the importance of employees; the expectations of stakeholders; and the road map to goal achievement and success. These are accompanied by postings that clearly lay out the company's goals and objectives. For example, ZiLOG has an important financial goal related to earnings before interest, taxes, depreciation, and amortization (EBITDA). To focus attention on this metric, a visually powerful graphic was developed so that employees could track the company's progress on a regular basis. This is shown in Figure 4-2.

Elsewhere, ZiLOG posts a series of charts that help to explain its core processes and the phases of its product development. In hallways, there are bulletin boards with many photos commemorating the company, its customers, and its employees. A core process map is prominently posted next to performance results. Project planning and developmental charts, known as the project pipeline, are physically posted and updated regularly in areas where project personnel will see them constantly. In hallways and entries, large framed photos of products remind employees and visitors of what ZiLOG does. The information available in these visuals is impressive in both amount and detail.

All of these information sets are linked to the bottom line in a comprehensive war room, centrally located for easy access by employees. The war room contains a series of charts that track financial data, customer and employee satisfaction, project performance, and financial results. Information displays are not limited to the war room, however. Other information is displayed throughout the physical plant using a combination of charts and clever graphics to engage all who see it. Job aids describing each step of a particular task are located at the bench or position where that task is performed. Team performance charts are kept at team work stations and updated regularly. Customer satisfaction displays are readily visible in customer-accessible areas, as well as in employee performance areas. Each per-

Figure 4-1. One panel from the ZiLOG employee communications board shows clearly that communication and information sharing are important here. The board has four panels, each of which reminds employees of what, when, and how to communicate effectively.

Figure 4-2. A quick glance at this powerful graphic tells the full story of how well employees at ZiLOG are meeting the company's EBITDA goal.

formance metric at ZiLOG is posted where there is the greatest opportunity to influence it.

Port Angeles School District

Another organization that uses visual displays in an integrated fashion is the Port Angeles School District in Port Angeles, Washington. There are components of visual management in many of the schools in this district, and the central administration is initiating the integration of visual management into its district operations during the 2003–2004 school year. One might expect to see lots of art in a school or school district office, but in Port Angeles the art is being integrated into key communication mechanisms that reflect the cultures of the schools and the community they serve. At one elementary school, for example, there is a historical time line posted in the lobby to commemorate the history of that school's development and growth. It is a constant reminder to students, teachers, and parents of the roots, history, and continuity of this school.

The sign on the front lawn of Port Angeles High School is a three-dimensional cutout that mirrors the Olympic Mountains behind the campus; the sign anchors the high school visually to its community and its surroundings, reminding us of the importance of place and community. Although Port Angeles High School is in the early stages of visual management development, faculty and students have enhanced some classrooms visually to clearly display and explain their purpose. Other preparations for visual management are underway. The main lobby of the high school is a large, bright, and open area. The space has been cleared of clutter, old and unmatched furnishings have been removed, the school's motto has been placed in a prominent position, and the walls are being prepared for new and exciting visuals. The lobby has become a work in progress, a clean slate upon which to craft an important part of the visual environment, and signals that something new is going on here.

Most schools in the district are still in the very early stages of considering or planning a visual management strategy to support their operating strategies. One elementary school, however, stands out as a wonderful example of how visual management can support and enhance an educational environment. Anyone who enters the Franklin Elementary School in Port Angeles knows that this facility is quite different from a traditional school building. The walls, the floors, the ceilings, and virtually every inch of available space are filled with charts, information, and artistic creations that literally leap out in three dimensions. Some of these represent core lessons, such as the reading score charts shown in Figure 4-3; some represent current and future learning activities, such as a totem tales display that students created as they learned about Northwest Coast natives. Many repre-

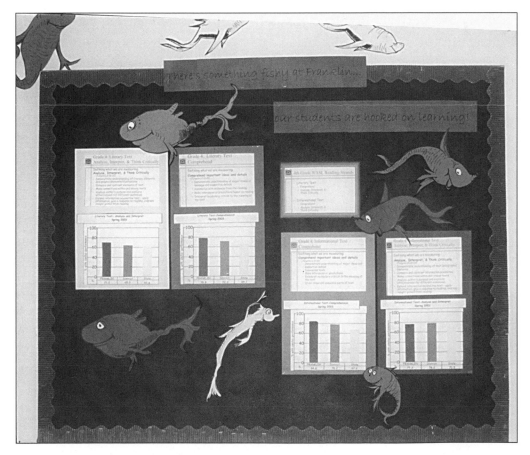

Figure 4-3. Bright, eye-catching graphics show the reading test score results of the Washington Assessment of Student Learning for Franklin students.

sent student and school achievements, and some reflect the values and attributes of the school. It is instantly clear that creativity is valued here, and that each child contributes to a continually evolving artistic scheme to teach, to share, and to inspire. The visuals both promote and reinforce this value.

A walk through the school shows highly motivated and energized children who are captivated by the school's design and culture and who are engaged in learning. The children have found ways to create visual displays that show what and how they are learning. They talk about and work toward the goals represented in the graphics, and they credit the visuals with helping them focus. Moreover, it is also readily apparent that the parents have bought into this approach and that they are actively involved in their children's education. Parents are seen in the school at all times of day: helping out in classrooms, reading to children in the central reading room–library, and working with children on projects and other work. Their contributions are noted in a variety of visuals throughout the school.

The Franklin School has a war room, like many businesses that have adopted visual management practices. Teachers and administrators use this war room to track performance at a variety of levels against the district and school goals. Performance charts are displayed in the school's war room and in other locations as well. The charts make it clear that the school is not using art for art's sake, but is using it as a tool to help improve the school's performance and, more important, the performance of its students. Even planning meetings at Franklin use visual management principles, as can be seen in Figure 4-4. Faculty and students see constant reminders of great work, strong performance, and progress toward goal achievement everywhere they look. It is difficult to be at Franklin and not catch "improvement fever."

At Franklin, as in so many other organizations, leadership has played an important role in the success of visual management. The principal and the teaching staff at this school are committed to achieving the goals set forth in the district's strategic plan, and they

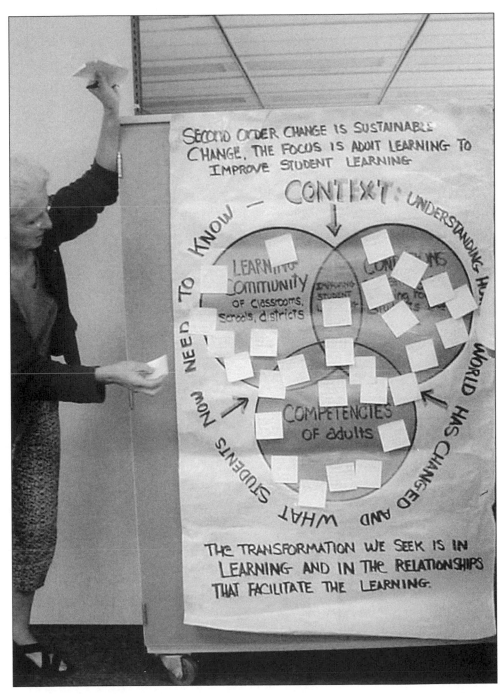

Figure 4-4. Visual management even permeates planning activities in the Port Angeles School District, as can be seen in this administrative meeting at Franklin.

use many visual mechanisms to remind themselves of what these goals are. Visual lesson plans, student and class progress charts, individual learning goals, class achievement charts, and schoolwide progress toward goal achievement are posted everywhere that there is wall or ceiling space. A mission/vision statement is prominently displayed at the main entry to the school, so that any visitor is instantly informed of what is important at this school. The principal and the teachers are also visible, always stopping to help a child or cheer a child on, going out of their way to congratulate a child or a colleague on a job well done, and showing off the latest achievements of their colleagues and students with great pride. The principal and the teachers know exactly where the school stands with respect to its goals every day; every teacher knows exactly where his classes stand and how each student has performed at all times. Because the data are available and visible, the leaders in this school know at all times what is expected of them and are better able to lead in the right direction.

QTC Medical Services, Inc.

QTC Medical Services, Inc., based in Diamond Bar, California, provides medical evaluations for disability-based benefit and insurance programs. Since 1981, QTC has conducted exams and prepared medical reports for government agencies, insurance companies, and employers throughout the United States. Visual management at QTC keeps employees and affiliates focused on the mission and goals of the organization. There are photos of customers throughout the facility, helping people remember the importance of those they serve. Employees, associates, customers, and visitors see constant reminders of the values and vision of this service business. One of these reminders is shown in Figure 4-5.

Employees and employee performance are critical at QTC, particularly because of the medical services it provides. The QTC war room contains the latest data about overall performance, as well as individual, team, and group results. The company shares information widely with employees, who check update boards frequently to see how their

Figure 4-5. Every person who enters the QTC offices in Diamond Bar, California, is greeted with this medical services organization's vision.

teams are doing, as can be seen in Figure 4-6. The wealth of performance data available to employees, the emphasis on performance, and the visual nature of much of this information reinforce high employee accountability and the results orientation of the organization. Visual management has helped improve communication and performance at QTC.

UltraViolet Devices, Inc.

UltraViolet Devices, Inc. (UVDI), is another California company that uses visual management. UVDI is headquartered in Santa Clarita and manufactures ultraviolet devices for a variety of industrial uses, including water purification systems. The company competes in the

Figure 4-6. Employees check update boards regularly at QTC to determine how they are doing and what the current priorities are.

areas of ultraviolet lamp fabrication technology, photocatalytic oxidation technology, semirobotic orbital and lathe welding capabilities, and manufacturing process controls. It is known as a world-class manufacturer and supplier of these technologies, with strong core competences in these areas.

Upon entering the facility, it is immediately apparent that employees are important to the company. One of the first things a visitor sees is the display case shown in Figure 4-7, which contains a small statue of every employee in the organization, including the president. These statues are surprisingly realistic and eye-catching. Each employee is given the same level of importance in this display, emphasizing UVDI's desire to treat people equally and to celebrate all employees.

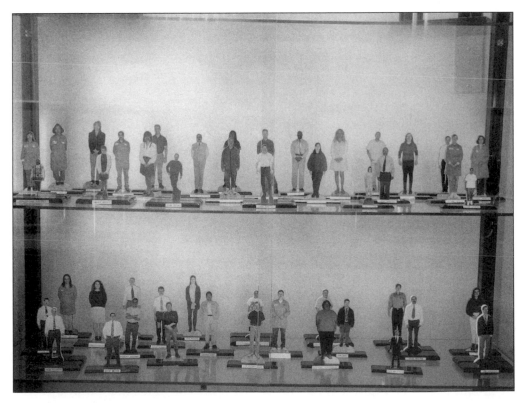

Figure 4-7. Statues of all employees greet visitors at UVDI. They reflect the company's ongoing commitment to the importance and value of its employees.

Inside the UVDI plant, the manufacturing floor is very neat, clean, and free from clutter, which is consistent with the Japanese 5-S process described in Chapter 3. Performance and technical information is posted on the manufacturing floor so that the employees know what to do, how to do it, and how they are doing at all times. Work instruction guides, also known as job aids, describing the operation are highly visual and are posted at each work station across the entire manufacturing process. These job aids show employees graphically how to correct common mistakes. Area performance data are posted in each work area and updated regularly. See Figure 4-8 for a typical view of the manufacturing floor. Note the performance chart to the right of the employee and the job aids to the right of that.

UVDI also uses other visuals throughout the organization that highlight its many successes, particularly those of the employees. Banners hang in the work areas to thank employees for work well done. Other visuals commend them for meeting targets. These visuals help to reinforce success and foster a sense of pride among the employees.

U.S. Department of Veterans Affairs

Another organization that has integrated visual management into its operations is the U.S. Department of Veterans Affairs (VA). The Los Angeles Regional Office (RO), for example, utilizes all the components of an advanced visual management organization, including a series of three-dimensional objects to help connect its employees to its mission of serving veterans. The Department of Veterans Affairs is housed on six floors of the Federal Building. Employees and visitors are greeted by a different display in the elevator lobby on each floor: a model of a World War I submarine, a vintage World War II jeep, a U-2 cockpit, a Huey helicopter, an Abrams M-1 tank, and the Civil War cannon shown in Figure 4-9. These artifacts, combined with the wall displays about veterans and the history of the VA, signal clearly what this place is all about. The breadth, depth, and magni-

Figure 4-8. *The manufacturing area at UVDI is brightly lit and clear of clutter. Employees post results regularly on the white board to the left of center in this photo, and job aids above the work stations at the right show employees exactly how to perform the operations required there.*

Figure 4-9. This Civil War cannon is one of a number of displays at the U.S. Department of Veterans Affairs that honor veterans for their service to the United States. It is a visually captivating way to remind all who see it that veterans are important in this place. (Photograph by Jason Gray.)

tude of the display tells you that something different is happening here.

At this RO, there are also replicas of a field hospital, the Vietnam Veterans Memorial, a bunker, and a prisoner-of-war cell to remind visitors and employees alike of the RO's critical focus on the veterans who are its customers. Military pictures adorn the walls, and the halls are peopled with life-size cutouts of veterans in uniform. For the visitor, this place is an astonishing museum, dedicated to the tens of thousands of veterans served by the office. Adults and children who visit are touched deeply by the VA's commitment to veterans. After one visit by a school group, for example, the children wrote thank-you letters to soldiers and veterans to show appreciation for their efforts. As you can see in Figure 4-10, the letters were mounted and publicly displayed for employees, veterans, and other visitors to read.

For the employees, however, it is a thriving, successful organization whose primary purpose is to grant benefits whenever possible to veterans who have earned them. This mission cannot be ignored: The road map to success shown in Figure 4-11 is posted prominently for all to see; huge photographs of veterans hang from the ceiling among banners proclaiming, "Grant when you can"; and the core values of the organization are posted prominently in many work areas. Constant visual reminders of the organization's purpose surround the employees, and they work harder than ever before to achieve their mission.

The casual visitor may not notice that the RO also maintains a series of war rooms that track performance data, and that it utilizes many flip charts and other displays to track daily performance indicators. The war rooms are important to the employees; the wall displays enable them to track performance data over time and know how they have been doing, as can be seen in Figure 4-12. War room data are reinforced by messages carried on television monitors located throughout the RO that track and report telephone performance, performance relative to monthly goals, and team rewards and recognition information. By surrounding themselves with up-to-date performance data, employees ensure that they are constantly aware of how their teams and the office overall are performing.

Employees are always a critical factor in the success of any organization, and the visual management firm celebrates them for their contributions to that success. The RO celebrates its employees in a variety of different ways. It has created an Employee Wall of Fame, where employees who have performed exceptionally well are honored. Throughout the halls of the RO, there are displays to remind people of the hard work that is being done in the various areas. Thank-you cards linked to the visual road map are provided to employees, who are expected to use them to thank others who have done good work or made a particularly appreciated contribution. In an area

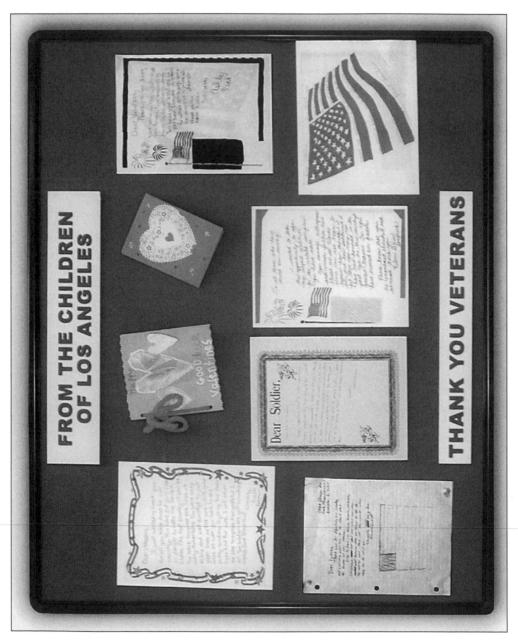

Figure 4-10. Children were so touched by the contributions of veterans that they wrote personal notes to soldiers and veterans to thank them for their bravery and sacrifices. (Photograph by Jason Gray.)

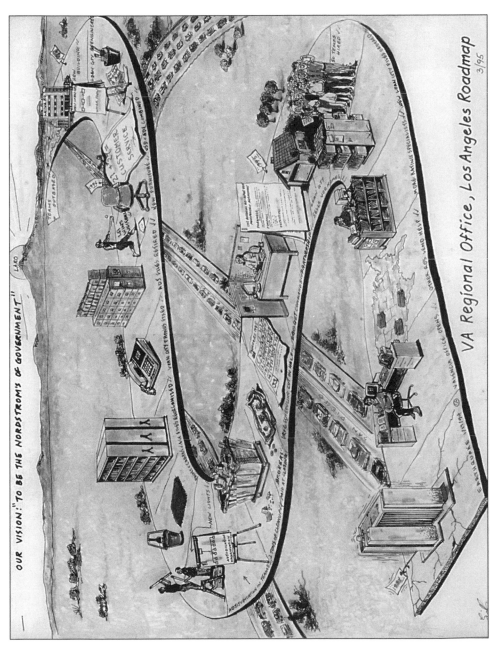

Figure 4-11. Visual management encourages organizations to develop and post personalized road maps to help keep the mission and vision in front of employees and visitors at all times.

Figure 4-12. Managers and employees check war room data displays regularly at the VA to stay abreast of performance to plan and to ensure they are meeting their goals. (Photograph by Jason Gray.)

known as the Employee Wing, there are sixteen panels filled with pictures of all the RO employees; this is shown in Figure 4-13. These tributes to employees were not developed overnight, yet they have had an electric impact on members of the RO, who now feel appreciated and recognized for their contributions.

Over the past nine years, the RO has been building a strong visual management environment. The changes that have been wrought in this office are astounding: They have dramatically altered the culture and contributed to a significant increase in customer satisfaction, timeliness, and accuracy.

Columbus Regional Hospital

Columbus Regional Hospital (CRH), located in Columbus, Indiana, has taken visual management principles to a different level with its

Figure 4-13. Celebrating employees takes a lot of wall space in the VA's Employee Wing, where photographs of all employees are displayed. (Photograph by Jason Gray.)

commitment to incorporating architecture, interior design, and heal-ing arts into its mission to improve the health and well-being of the people it serves. In 1990, ground was broken for a major renovation and expansion program. The leaders of the hospital and of this proj-ect determined that healing involved more than simply technology or medicine, and they created an environment that incorporated art and design into the business framework. The existing buildings were reno-vated in the Prairie style of Frank Lloyd Wright and were then united with the new space in a consistent design that captured a sense of history at the same time that it built a modern medical campus. The colors were carefully selected to be inviting and soothing, and the interior space was designed to make movement about the facility easy. Lighting, too, was provided to best suit the various purposes of each area.

The lobby, reminiscent of that of a nice hotel, is warm and com-fortable. It reflects many of the unifying visual themes of the design of the campus, as can be seen in Figure 4-14. Fine art is hung through-out the campus as part of the healing arts program, but the real visual management elements focus on the business of the hospital and its mission to its stakeholders. In the hallways and wings, display boards tell the stories of how people are working here. "Superstar" boards for the various service areas publicly highlight exceptional service providers, white boards are used for information sharing and schedul-ing, and posters celebrating employee accomplishments abound. Yet art for the sake of art is not what this regional hospital is all about. The art is a reminder of and a support mechanism for a very specific mission and set of business goals. Even unit performance is tracked with a visual component, as can be seen in Figure 4-15. At Columbus Regional Hospital, visual management permeates everything that is done.

■ What Is Different in These Visual Management Organizations?

The examples just given provide a glimpse into several organizations that are at different stages of evolution with regard to visual manage-

Figure 4-14. Columbus Regional Hospital's lobby has been designed to enhance the peace and comfort of those who enter. It reflects the Prairie style of the surrounding area, creates a sense of almost homelike comfort, and reinforces employee pride in the organization. There is no institutional atmosphere here. Rather, the architecture and interior design are used to create a healing environment.

ment. All of them are well managed, all are improving their performance with the implementation of visual management, and all are striving to become the best they can be. They have strong leaders, well-designed operating systems, clear missions and goals, appropriate technology, well-trained and competent employees, strong and fair human resource practices, and access to the necessary resources to carry out their missions. These are the fundamentals of sound management and the building blocks for success in any organization.

What is different about visual management organizations is a matter of degree and scope: In a visual management environment,

Figure 4-15. This employee at Columbus Regional Hospital is updating a performance display board used to recognize staff members of one medical-surgical department who make a difference in improving patient satisfaction. The board also communicates to patients and employees that CRH is working hard to make sure their needs are met during their hospitalization.

all of the design and performance elements are tied closely together through careful organization design coupled with new, visual, and highly visible communication mechanisms. The organization design elements (the prevailing technology, the formal and informal organizational structure, the information and communication systems, the human resource systems, the reward systems, and the renewal systems) are more tightly aligned using fine arts principles, and they are much more visible for all to see and understand.

People are connected to the mission on a much deeper level because of the power of images, and this influences the culture of the organization in powerful ways. In the mid-1990s, for example, the Los

Angeles VA Regional Office had a very conservative culture and denied benefits at a higher rate than the rest of the nation. Once the RO made it clear that granting benefits was the priority, then reinforced this message through banners, pictures, flags, videos, and dioramas reminding employees to grant whenever they could, the grant rates rose until they reached appropriate levels. Using visual images as vehicles for immediate communication, the RO reinforced the core message of its mission and influenced employee performance to a measurable degree.

In a visual management organization, employees are provided with a degree of information that they have not previously had, linking them more closely to the metrics than anyone had previously thought possible. UVDI, for example, typically hires employees at relatively low wage rates. Despite this, the employees are all taught the metrics and required to report performance data on a half-hourly or hourly basis. All of the data are recorded and posted at the work site, then they are rolled up and posted on a centralized bulletin board the following day for everyone to see. Employees' pay is directly linked to organizational performance, and employees take an active interest in learning the metrics and trying to improve that performance.

In addition to the direct performance gains seen with the advent of visual management, we find that the physical plant becomes so interesting and compelling that it serves as an impressive recruitment and retention tool. Federal employees in high-cost areas in the United States are paid about 40 percent less than their counterparts in the private sector. This makes recruitment of talented people very difficult for most federal agencies located in these areas. Because several of the VA regional offices are filled with examples of the sacrifices of veterans, prospective employees, who are given tours of the physical plant during the interview process, are struck by the opportunity to make a difference in the lives of others. The visual environment grabs those individuals who are looking for the opportunity to be a part of something bigger than themselves, and they develop a strong desire to work in such an organization. It is clear that articulation of the mission, core values, and performance goals has a dramatic impact on these prospective employees, and that the practice of visual management enables these offices to compete for talent in tight markets.

Finally, the images throughout these organizations are so powerful that they strongly and positively influence the outside world's view of them. A local congressman visited the Federal Building in one of the high-cost areas in order to meet and greet the agencies located there. He spent about five minutes each with most of the agencies, but he spent an entire hour with the VA regional office. When he finished his visit, he said, "I'm glad to see there is at least one agency here that knows who its customers are." The visual management environment reshaped his view of the regional office in a positive manner. In the same manner, the Franklin School in Port Angeles, Washington, influences visitors and the outside world with its visual management and messaging. One cannot help but see the importance of teaching and learning in this environment. Vibrant wall displays celebrate students and staff and serve as reminders of core values, as seen in Figure 4-16. These are clear examples of the power of the visual management environment in influencing the outside world's perspective of the organization.

■ How Does It Work?

You may be wondering at this point how and why this all works. You may agree that this really does make a place look better but still be trying to understand why the visuals drive performance improvements. The reason visual management works is that it is real, it is constant, it permeates the organization with a culture of performance, and it appeals directly to employees whose environments contribute to short attention spans and a need for nearly constant mental stimulation. Visual management's focus on mission and performance keeps people moving in the right direction, and its emphasis on training and education helps to consistently reinforce the organization's needs.

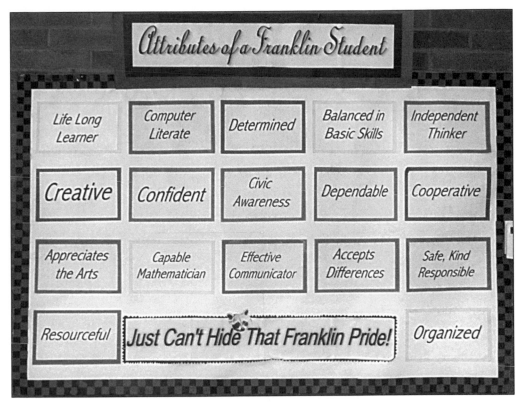

Figure 4-16. In the Franklin School lobby, students, staff, and visitors are constantly reminded of what it means to be a student here.

Mission

Displays that deal with the organization's mission are designed to connect the employees to that mission, so that they are excited and intrigued by it, and therefore feel emotional about it. These displays are updated periodically to maintain heightened interest and to avoid the staleness that so often results from lack of change. How often do you or other employees at your place of work check bulletin boards or other areas where information is posted? In the visual management environment, people check them frequently, since the information is updated and changed regularly. People know where to look for information because they have been carefully introduced to the information, shown where it will be, and trained to use it in their daily activities. In fact, in some visual management transformations, leaders have given employees tours to help them understand what is being done, how it all fits together, and why it is being done. We find that when employees are armed with such information, many of them want to be involved in the creative transformation process and contribute in new and meaningful ways. As a result, they have a greater and deeper understanding of all the displays, and they tend to use the information to better advantage. The emotional connection helps them focus on what they are in business to do.

Think about the primary mission of your organization. Do you provide health-care services, manufacture industrial goods, or produce consumer goods? Do you deliver financial services, provide educational or training services, administer government programs, or conduct research? Are you a government contractor, in the hospitality industry, or in the retail sector? How would you characterize your mission? What is your vision of the process of accomplishing that mission? Each type of organization just mentioned may have a very different mission statement from the rest, yet there will be a great deal of commonality among them. The common ground is that all organizations, whatever their form, have internal and external stakeholders, customers, systems, and strategies.

No matter what the arena in which you work may be, there is a mission that should be guiding all activities and performance. Most missions connect directly to the customer, all are noble, and all can hook people and make them feel proud of their organization, but the mission must be clear and explicit and meaningful in order to energize people to try to accomplish it. As people begin to identify with the mission and vision of their organization, they begin to see just how they contribute to its outcomes, and their behavior begins to change. But before these behavioral changes occur, people need to see and feel the reality of the mission. They also need to understand the core values that will guide behavior and performance. That is why the mission statement in visual management organizations is a document in which images count more than words, and the walls, lobbies, ceilings, and work areas are all viewed as opportunities to reflect the mission and connect employees to their customers, not merely as pleasantly designed areas where the organization's employees work.

Customers typically feel celebrated in visual management organizations. The mission statements and goals reflect a direct customer focus, the displays introduce and highlight what customers do and want, customer feedback and survey data are prominently posted for all to see, and it becomes clear that the customer is central to the organization's success. At Columbus Regional Hospital, for example, an exemplary history wall has been developed that depicts the organization's roots and transitions, from its birth in 1915 as Bartholomew County Hospital, through acceptance of its first patients in 1917, to its current status as a major regional health-care provider system. The wall, shown in Figure 4-17, re-creates the history of Columbus Regional Hospital for all who view it, showing the importance of roots,

Figure 4-17. This photo of the original building at Columbus Regional Hospital shows how far it has come since its founding and helps patients, visitors, and employees see its tradition of service and commitment to excellent health care. (Photograph by Mike Dickbernd, *The Republic,* 333 Second St., Columbus, IN 47201.)

community, and people to its current success. As the Columbus Regional Hospital story shows, customers as well as employees are connected to the mission in the visual management environment.

Employee Focus

As well as connecting people to the mission, the physical environment also projects a great deal of information and includes many displays about the organization's employees. One mistake that organizations often make is to become so focused on the customer that they lose sight of the people who are serving that customer: the employees. A true visual management environment has all sorts of displays relating to the employees: celebratory posters and displays, personal artifacts, newsletters, employee-of-the-quarter programs, photos of the employees' children, and advertisements of various employee events. An organization may even have a gallery of employee artwork. Figure 4-18 shows one way in which Columbus Regional Hospital celebrates its employees.

This emphasis on the employee is an important component of visual management. Such a visual emphasis reinforces employees' connection to the mission and helps them understand that their employer is proud of them and truly cares about them. In this environment, employees really want to give back. They feel connected and appreciated, and their level of satisfaction begins to rise. Their energy level rises, their number of grievances and complaints declines because they feel proud of what they are doing, and they feel that the organization truly cares about them and wants to help them. Once that happens, we begin to see that more satisfied employees begin to provide better service, as is suggested in the research about the link between employees who feel connected to their work and the bottom-line results. Yet there is another issue to consider when assessing the value of this link.

Performance Metrics

Leaders in organizations frequently decide to share performance data with the employees in an effort to boost performance; they have

Figure 4-18. When a staff member in surgical services at Columbus Regional Hospital is singled out for extraordinary service in a patient satisfaction survey, his or her name is proudly added to the Surgical Services Superstar board for all to see.

learned from observation and research that there is a link between employees' knowing how the unit is doing and their subsequent performance. Too often, however, they distribute balance sheets and other financial information and expect employees to be able to read and understand this information, translate it into measures that are meaningful to them, and then use it to highlight areas for improvement. Such leaders often do not ensure that employees have a clear understanding of the organization's performance metrics, and without this understanding, employees find it difficult to utilize the data in any meaningful way.

Yet metrics are important. Metrics are the performance indicators that organizations use to determine how they are doing. While the specific metrics vary from organization to organization and from level to level within an organization, the broad metrics are usually similar and include various cost, quality, and delivery performance measures. In a manufacturing environment, these metrics would probably include direct and indirect material costs, labor costs, a host of product quality measures, and on-time-delivery measures. In a phone center, the metrics might include the number of calls handled in a particular time period, the average length of a call, the wait time to connect, and transaction completion rates. A loan-processing center might use such metrics as conversion rates (ratio of loans granted to applications), write-offs, and processing costs. Retailers would definitely look at shrinkage, sales dollars per employee, overhead, average sale per customer or employee, and a variety of customer satisfaction measures, including repeat business.

Unfortunately, metrics such as these are often not well understood below the senior management level. In too many organizations, supervisors and other employees do not understand how to interpret these data or how their individual performance contributes to the bottom line. This is unacceptable in a visual management organization, where the metrics are posted for all to see and everyone is trained to understand and use them.

In the visual management environment, data are posted to an unprecedented degree and in a variety of formats: They are seen on bulletin boards, in war rooms, on television monitors, and in other displays. But that's only the beginning, and, in fact, it doesn't do much unless management takes the time to teach employees about the metrics. Simply posting information is not enough. It will not become meaningful to the employees unless management is committed to teaching the employees what it means, where it comes from, how it is calculated, and how it relates to them. However, a concerted effort to do this, coupled with tying the metrics to rewards, will pay big dividends over time. In the long run, the employees will not only see the importance of the metrics, but begin to relate them to the other visuals, such as the mission and customer displays, resulting in a higher employee commitment level than was initially thought possible. Once employees understand the metrics, they begin to see the big picture at the individual, team, and system levels, and they begin to become more connected to the work of the organization. But even that is not enough. These metrics must still be made real to the employees.

In addition to posting the metrics, leaders in a visual management organization take great care to determine the appropriate degree of detail for each employee level. The front-line employees, for example, see metrics that relate to their own work posted in their areas; in many cases, individual performance may be posted. These employees know that they have a personal impact on these particular metrics, and they have been taught what these metrics mean and how they are calculated. Once metrics have been taught to employees, and once we have ensured that the metrics are geared to what's important to employee performance, then these key metrics can be tied to formal or informal rewards. Progress toward such rewards, whether they are formal bonuses or informal recognition such as coffee or lunches, is posted and updated regularly so that all employees can see just how they are doing relative to the goals and the resulting reward and/or recognition. This helps ensure the employees' interest in achieving the organization's goals. The metrics may be posted in a variety of different ways ranging from flip charts to grease boards, from computers to television monitors. The key is that they must have meaning for the employees' immediate work, be clear and understandable, and be ultimately linked to some form of reward.

The more the rewards are linked to the metrics at the team level, the more people will pay attention to the metrics and the more they will focus their energy on achieving the organization's goals. Therefore, we must not only teach the metrics, but also ensure that people understand the reward system. This system must be visible, and data related to it must be updated as frequently as possible so that employees get real-time information that they can use. The link between metrics and rewards should be reinforced through training, discussion, and other means so that employees cannot ignore the performance-reward link. This link really helps them focus on the organization and its goals.

A broader range of metrics is typically posted in one or more war rooms to enable mid-level and upper-level management to spot trends and to analyze an overall balanced series of measures. These metrics cover all the important measures of success for the organization and give a complete picture of the current state of performance. At the employee level, a more simplified version of these metrics is posted that relates directly to the team members and the work they produce. As the organization matures, more and more of the lower-level employees are introduced to the war room and can begin to see how the measures relate. This helps them learn about their contribution to the bigger picture, and once they have learned which measures they can directly affect, employees tend to focus their efforts even more clearly in appropriate areas.

Posting the metrics throughout the organization in different forms and teaching these metrics to the employees ensures that dozens of eyes are always examining organizational performance. This virtually guarantees that performance will receive greater internal scrutiny than ever before, and it results in more ideas and effort to improve the organization being put forward. In essence, the way in which front-line employees perceive themselves and their contributions to the organization begins to change significantly; they move from seeing themselves as single, independent workers to seeing themselves as individuals who work together toward a common set of goals, and they begin to think more like managers then ever before. Having constant knowledge of how they are doing is a great reinforcement for improving employees' performance.

Education and Training

One last element is making sure that we give employees the necessary tools to achieve the metrics, the goals, and the rewards. We do this through education and training. Well-trained employees are a must for any organization. Too many organizations today rely primarily on written material for training and education, even though research indicates that different people learn in different ways. In fact, literature on engineering education shows that nearly two-thirds of students learn best if they are actively involved in the learning process, and that more than two-thirds are visual learners.[3,4] These findings suggest that the visual management environment, which encourages visual and interactive training, will be very effective in ensuring that employees get the greatest benefit from training designed to improve their skills.

Beyond the traditional series of materials and training classes utilized to make sure we teach the employees the skills needed for their work, though, we advocate the development of learning maps for all key processes. Learning maps can be used to lay out visually all the key processes in an organization. They help us create job aids (workflow charts) that we can post throughout the workplace to give employees much more information about the work, much more control over their learning processes, and many more tools for learning the job. This helps them to improve their accuracy, reduce the number of bottlenecks in the process, better understand what is required in order to succeed, and work to reduce the amount of rework. Learning maps help employees achieve the organization's goals because they clarify visually what is needed and help employees understand how everything fits together. Critical information is at employees' fingertips in a visual manner that fits perfectly with what they see in everyday life. Learning maps help reduce the information overload that feeds poor performance.

A final, and important, note about education in organizations has to do with the way in which the physical spaces for meeting and learning are improving. Herrmann International, a firm that specializes in conducting research about how people think and learn and applying that research in work environments, has become well known for its learning center in Lake Lure, North Carolina. This space has been designed as a visual feast: Color, texture, and shape have all been utilized to make the space vibrant and alive. It is filled with objects that enhance learning and playfulness, and that are used to stimulate and engage the people who come here to meet and learn. The learning center was developed and designed with the concepts of visual learning and visual literacy in mind, and it has been a tremendous success because of this attention to how people learn best.

■ Love the Pictures, but What About Performance?

Visual management is first and foremost about performance. It is not about interior design, it is not about making people feel good, and it is certainly not about posting a bunch of information. It is a system that reinforces tried-and-true management principles and techniques through the use of fine arts techniques. While we sometimes see organizations using several visual elements, these elements often are not used in a synchronized and purposeful way. Visual management takes these disconnected visual elements and organizes them in a logical, cohesive manner to promote that elusive "culture" that virtually every manager strives to attain. In essence, visual management rallies people around the mission and the metrics in order to produce highly motivated employees. The more people understand the mission, recognize its importance, and feel proud of it, the more they will want to take the extra step toward achieving it. The more they understand the metrics, recognize their importance, and try to influence them, the better the organization will perform.

Individual Performance

It is generally accepted that a talented, well-trained, and motivated workforce will be high performing. A visual management organization helps attract and keep such a workforce because the environment is designed to support a culture of high performance. Jon Katzenbach, in his book *Peak Performance*, suggests that the way to improve employee motivation and increase employee performance is by engaging an emotional commitment by the employees to the organization. According to Katzenbach, this emotional engagement can occur through the directed use of mission, vision, and values; through the application of metrics to enhance accountability; through internal entrepreneurship; through pay-for-performance schema; and/or through recognition and celebration of employee accomplishments.[5] The visual management workplace relies on mechanisms in each of these areas to engage the workforce in the ongoing mission of the organization.

The visual management workplace is visually attractive, coordinated in design, neat, uncluttered, and easy to navigate. Signage and all other visual displays send a message of focus, vibrancy, purpose, commitment, and coordination, all related to the organization's mission. Metrics are posted prominently, rewards are linked to performance, and employees are celebrated for their contributions and membership. The visuals make hard work more fun. Potential employees who visit a visual management office will actually feel the dynamic, high-performance culture and usually tell us that they want to be a part of it.

Once people become part of a visual management organization, they are treated well by that organization. Employees receive frequent recognition through employee celebrations, employee walls of fame, gifts, and awards of various monetary and nonmonetary types. High-performing individuals and teams find their pictures hung on the walls and their success stories posted next to the pictures, for all to see and learn from. They may be featured in internal newsletters or in videos that are produced to reinforce the power of their success stories. Often they are asked to represent the organization at meetings or conferences and to tell their stories. Some organizations create thank-you cards that include pictures of the organization's road map; these are given to employees in appreciation for good work, and the recipients are often encouraged to post them for all to see. Strong performance is recognized and rewarded in visual management organizations.

At the same, visual management recognizes that virtually every organization has low-performing employees. Sometimes these employees don't know that they are low performers and simply function as if they were on cruise control. When individual performance is posted for all to see, these individuals are first shocked and then embarrassed, because they do not want to feel pressure from their peers because of their low performance. As a result, they will often quickly improve their performance so that they will not be outliers within the group.

The other type of poor performer is the individual who simply can't do the job—and knows it. Sometimes these employees are angry because they have many problems outside the job that prevent them from focusing on the job, and sometimes they are simply incompetent and will never be able to do the job. As a result, they are either always badmouthing the organization because they blame it for their personal problems or trying to keep as low a profile as possible so that they will not be noticed, or both. In a visual management organization, these individuals are quickly identified and must be quickly dealt with. Not only is individual performance posted, as the sample chart in Figure 4-19 shows (usually on an anonymous basis, although everyone quickly figures out who the low performers are), but monthly report cards are issued to each employee that clearly state how that employee is doing. Problem employees are quickly identified and placed on notice. A good-faith effort is made to help them, but if this fails, appropriate action is taken.

This accomplishes a number of things, each of which helps to improve performance. First, all employees understand that they will be held accountable for their actions and performance. Second, supervisors learn that they, too, are accountable for employees' performance and that they will not be able to protect poor performers. Third, the performance bar actually rises because the bottom tier of employees feels peer pressure to improve. Fourth, employees begin to take greater notice of the posted metrics because they begin to see the connection between individual performance and group performance. As they get to know the linkages, they learn where to put forth their best efforts for performance improvement. Finally, morale improves, since the top performers are no longer frustrated because

Employee Name	Output*	Accuracy	Hours in Attendance**
A	4.65	91%	161
B	3.24	77%	142
C	6.25	83%	142
D	5.91	88%	123
E	2.28	63%	151
F	3.37	79%	160
G	4.59	89%	149
H	7.02	90%	157
I	4.07	81%	132
J	3.98	83%	149
K	3.32	81%	149
L	3.90	85%	129
M	2.91	72%	101
N	3.73	80%	151

*Units produced per day
**Hours in attendance per month

Figure 4-19. Posting individual results can be a powerful tool for improving performance. However, do not post individual results, even without attribution, as in this example, unless you plan to help employees improve their performance. If employees feel you are posting results for punitive reasons, it can create real morale and performance problems.

low performers are not being dealt with. This helps build credibility with all employees because everyone is treated equally and knows that performance will be measured by the numbers rather than by personalities. The net result of all this is that a clear message is sent to employees telling them that successful performance will be rewarded and that there are consequences for poor performance. We find that as a result, the employees strive to improve and organizational performance moves upward.

Role of Leadership

While some may disagree, it has been our experience that the single most important component of a successful organization is its leadership. Good leaders will change bad systems and make them work better. Conversely, bad leaders will slowly but surely undermine good systems until they become misaligned and misused. Visual management will not work well in an organization with bad leaders; strong leadership is a key component of the success of visual management. Even an organization that is filled with good leaders will stumble with visual management if these leaders don't believe in the concept. However, if an organization has good leaders who want to move the organization to a higher level of performance, who are not afraid to let their management systems drive the organization instead of overrelying on heroic management, who create an environment that is attractive while constantly reinforcing the overall management philosophy and core values, and who want to lead an organization that is just plain "cool," then visual management is the way to go.

Visual management drives a significant cultural change in most organizations. Leaders in today's organizations are challenged to lead effective change—change both in performance and in culture and behavior. The visual management organization confronts its leaders with these challenges of change on a daily basis. In fact, the leaders' role is pivotal in ensuring that visual management gains a foothold and grows in an organization.

Great leaders also know that they can't do it alone. They must surround themselves with other leaders who share similar philosophies and values. Consistency of belief is critical to a well-led organization. Styles may differ among leaders—in fact, they probably should—but leaders must share common values, fully support a common mission, and work together toward common goals. Inconsistencies among leaders, lack of common purpose, and the perception of individual agendas create frustration and confusion among employees, and can quickly undermine a leader's credibility. Therefore, it must be clearly understood that before an organization can be transformed into a visual management environment, it must work to develop a cohesive management team that is dedicated to taking the organization to another level of performance.

Once the management team is lined up and committed, it will find that visual management makes its job easier because the employees, no matter how diverse the group, will become united behind the mission and the metrics. Employees at all levels who are surrounded by visual reminders of the mission and the metrics cannot readily ignore or avoid them. With solid leadership to guide the transformation to a visual management environment in a coherent manner, employees have a clear path to follow. This does not happen overnight, and it requires a significant amount of time and effort. However, leadership that is united in mission and purpose can ensure that successes begin to flow from the visual management transformation, and that employees join the process.

■ The Transparency of Core Processes

Because involvement is so important to the success of the initiative, we must fully engage employees in the visual management process. This requires that employees see, feel, and understand fully the processes of which they are a part and to which they contribute. In visual management, we work to create transparency of core processes to enhance this understanding.

The graphic displays in visual management organizations are not random. Each has a clear purpose and function. All visuals are designed to be informative, and many are designed to be directly educational. In general, those displays that provide information about the actual work flows and processes are designed to ensure that anyone on site can understand what is happening at any stage of the work process. Because each individual member of the organization is expected to understand the full core process of the organization, transparency of process is important for top performance.

The Value of Transparent Processes

A finished product or service is generally a function of the collective efforts of many people utilizing a series of different processes. People are usually familiar with one or two processes, but they are rarely familiar with all of the processes or with how those processes fit together to create the finished product or service that is the core mission of the organization. Large manufacturing and assembly plants are rife with stories of long-term employees who have never seen or entered areas of the plant other than their own. Today's networked organizations can exacerbate this challenge of understanding distant processes, since some parts of the work process are often located in another geographic area. Employees who do not understand the entire work process can create variances or errors that cost companies time and money through delays and rework. Moreover, the less familiar employees are with all of the processes, the less flexible the organization will be in reacting to the inevitable changes and improvements that the employees are required to make.

This is why visual management organizations seek to make their processes transparent, so that each employee understands the overall process and her contribution to it. We cannot achieve this by asking employees to read and retain all the information in complex technical manuals that contain hundreds of written pages; this would simply add to the information overload with which they already must cope.

A better approach is to create simplified diagrams and/or drawings of the processes and post them in the appropriate areas of the organization. Such learning maps are key tools of visual management. While these learning map diagrams and drawings may not contain as much detail as a technical manual, they will give employees a broad overview of the core processes. The UVDI core process diagrams and work instruction charts are good examples of technically complex processes that have been visually simplified for ease of understanding; one of the work instruction charts is shown in Figure 4-20. If more detail is needed than is given in these diagrams, employees can always turn to the technical manual or to a subject matter expert for more specific answers to technical questions.

The important lesson is to make the core processes transparent enough for employees to have a clear understanding of the steps in the process and to begin to see how its components fit together. This

Generation II	**UVDI WORK INSTRUCTION**	HCL2EG2-WI-7
09-1002	Enclosure Assembly, Station 7	Rev. A

Process Steps

	Process Steps	Actions			Quality Criteria	N.C.'s and Reaction Plans
Safety	*WEAR SAFETY GLASSES*					
010	Pick up a third switch. Install purple jumper between switch 2 and switch 3 per picture				Ensure insert tightly to switch	ITSS and see key person
020	Install ballast white wire to switch 3.				Ensure insert tightly to switch	ITSS and see key person
030	Install third switch into enclosure base using tool				Ensure that the switch is tight and secured	ITSS and see key person

Figure 4-20. At UVDI, a work instruction chart explains each step of the process (including safety requirements) for each manufacturing job, shows each step in a photo, explains the quality criteria for the operation, and lists other actions required to complete the job successfully.

level of understanding drives increased employee sensitivity to potential upstream and downstream errors and promotes teamwork across operations. Moreover, it helps employees relate all components of the core processes to the organization's metrics, and thus to become more engaged in actually trying to help manage the organization and its performance. Detailed and specific knowledge of and expertise in particular tasks or operations is required in order to get the job done well, but the value of this expertise is enhanced by a thorough understanding of the whole process.

Ensuring That Everyone Has the Skills and Knowledge to Do What Is Required

If employees don't have the skills to get the job done, it won't get done. It's that simple. Accordingly, every organization strives to develop a training plan that provides its employees with the skills they need if they are to get the job done. Too often, though, training is not done in a systematic fashion and seems to be given short shrift as a result of other work management priorities.

A visual management organization supports continuous training efforts by making the core processes obvious for all to see, by teaching its employees the performance metrics, and by using a wide variety of methodologies to make learning interesting and informative; learning maps, flowcharts, job aids, computer-based training, and videos are only a few of the visual and interactive tools used for training today. In short, a visual management organization will use many creative training approaches in the belief that anything that can be done to make training more attractive and to consistently reinforce its message is a good way to train.

Working Transparently

If properly applied, visual management makes many of the work processes and systems transparent. Information on these processes is not hidden away in books, in binders, or in the minds of subject-matter experts or upper management. It is open to whoever has a need for it and would like to know about it. Moreover, because people are more connected to the organization's mission and to the metrics, a growing number of individuals will want to know about more processes than ever before.

When one walks around a visual management organization, one can see people working, since they work in an open environment rather than behind large partitions. Work areas and work flow are clearly labeled, so everyone knows the where, why, and how of the process. Work in progress is located in highly visible areas for all to see: In visual management, it is important that everyone be able to actually see how things are going. This allows people to determine whether there are backlogs that need attention or whether work is being ignored. Core leaders walk around the organization and interact freely with the employees, which builds in another level of information flow. Leaders who are consistently scanning the work environment can gather a great deal of information from the body language of employees as well as from a scan of the work processes. This additional information helps them provide appropriate and helpful feedback as they walk about. Performance data are posted throughout the work area so that everyone knows how the organization is doing. Information, which is the most common source of power in an organization, is transferred from a few key individuals to as many people as possible, making the organization as a whole more powerful than ever.

■ Turning Employees On with Core Values

The last decade of corporate scandal has emphasized a growing need for strong organizational values, and these values are becoming more and more crucial to basic survival in today's business environment. Employees, customers, and other stakeholders are concerned with the activities of managers and leaders in both large and small organizations. In the wake of front-page headlines announcing the latest corporate wrongdoings, people are questioning organizational ethics and behavior to a greater degree than ever before. In response to such concerns, virtually every organization is developing a mission, vision, and core values statement. The real question is whether these statements are merely words or whether they truly reflect what the organization is all about.

We have all seen organizations develop mission statements, hand them out to employees, and post them in their lobbies for visitors to see. After a while, however, it seems that no one refers to them or even sees them anymore. A visual management organization, in contrast, creates a compelling set of core values, makes these values real to all employees, and continually reinforces its message over time. It takes the time to create a compelling poster that reinforces the words visually. A copy of the poster is given to every employee to post in his work area, and the poster is displayed throughout the organization.

When one of the VA's regional offices first developed its road map incorporating core values, the image was so compelling that virtually everyone hung it up in her workspace, copies were sent to stakeholders across the United States, and it wound up being published in Japan as a great example of vision and values. The Columbus Regional Hospital 2003–2004 strategic plan document, shown in Figure 4-21, also incorporates the organization's core values in a visual and visible manner.

A compelling image in and of itself will not change an organization's culture or enhance its values. For that to happen, the organization, particularly its leaders, must live the values every day. If leaders walk the talk, employees will follow, and the words and images on the wall will become symbols of pride and guidelines for behavior. In fact, when decisions or issues that involve core values come to the forefront, great leaders typically refer employees back to the images and

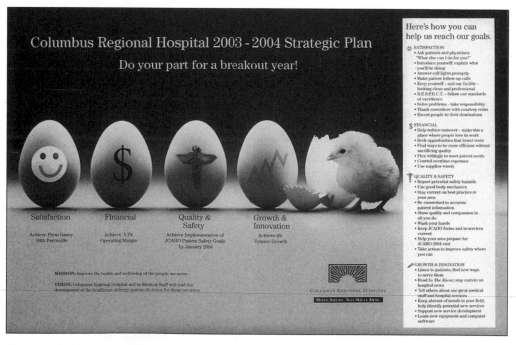

Figure 4-21. Columbus Regional Hospital used bright, simple, and clever graphics to breathe life into its strategic plan. It is difficult to miss the goals and core values that support this plan.

words on the wall, so that they know that the values are truly words by which to live.

Core values must also be made visible in displays other than the core values statement in order to ensure that they permeate the visual management environment. For example, if one of the core values is "employees are our greatest asset" but there are no employee displays throughout the organization, are employees really going to believe that they are valued? The point is that in a visual management organization, every visual design element should reflect the company's values. Thus, the core values become part of the fabric of work in that organization and will be ongoing drivers of behavior and performance.

Key Lessons from Visual Management Organizations

There are several core lessons to take away from this discussion that will enhance an understanding of the visual management organization.

Lesson 1: There's Only One Chance to Make a First Impression

First impressions are extremely powerful. When we meet someone for the first time, the initial impression we form seems to stay with us forever. The same thing happens when we visit an organization. We quickly sense the organizational climate; we feel whether the place has a sense of urgency; we seem to know whether it is a conservative or a liberal organization; we intuitively determine whether creativity is valued. The first impressions formed by visitors go a long way toward shaping the outside world's view of an organization. Since people today have so little time to really examine the facts, first impressions become sound bites: They're repeated frequently, and they often form an organization's external reputation. What first impression do visitors to your facility have? What kind of impression would you like to make?

People who visit a visual management organization are often captivated by the scope of the overall design. They immediately become hooked on the visual displays, since they sense that this is something they have not seen before. As they continue to tour the office, they note an overwhelming customer focus, the energy and enthusiasm of the employees, and a single-minded commitment to the bottom line. These visitors take away some of the excitement of the visual management environment and have a positive impression of the organization. They quickly realize that the organization has a clear purpose, knows its customers intimately, and has chosen a direction to follow in order to meet its goals.

Lesson 2: Make Sure the Environment Breathes the Customer

The visual management organization derives some of its success from focusing so clearly on the customer as a core facet of its mission. Mission and vision statements highlight the importance of internal and external customers, visual displays throughout the physical site depict and celebrate customers, and goals and metrics are directly tied to customer service. In fact, an environment that does not breathe the customer is not a very effective visual management environment because the customer is so central to good management and improved performance.

It is apparent that the Department of Veterans Affairs celebrates its customers, as the figures in this chapter have shown. Other companies, too, ensure that employees and visitors alike know and understand the importance of the customer to the business. Burbank Airport, in Burbank, California, has created many displays celebrating its customers and linking them to its flight services. Wall displays celebrate its partnership with Lockheed and show historical photos of the P-38 aircraft that were built there by Lockheed; other displays, like the one in Figure 4-22, celebrate the centennial of flight; and all incorporate customers as a key theme. Displays such as these reinforce the critical message that customers are important and help keep employees focused on appropriate goals.

Lesson 3: Always Celebrate Employees

There is no single resource in any organization that is more important than the organization's people, and a visual management environment is no exception. Visual management always celebrates employees as the primary drivers of performance and performance improvement. This improvement may be the result of physical effort, technological advances, or creative solutions to organizational challenges. Employees are the core of any organization; their work effort is crucial to its success, and strategies to acknowledge their efforts and to recognize and reward their performance are important for short- and long-term success.

In visual management, we celebrate employees in many ways to ensure that they feel appreciated, that they feel they are part of the system, and that they know how their achievements contribute to success. Employees who feel appreciated, who are valued members of the system, and who know how they contribute are more likely to want to stay in a particular organization and to contribute to its success. So, celebrations of employees can help with recruitment and retention in the visual management organization. They also can help motivate employees to continue to learn, to contribute in new ways, and to feel valued for doing so.

A recent survey on worker loyalty suggests that organizations should be encouraged to build a sense of camaraderie, team spirit, and pride into their organizations because employees who feel this sense of pride and spirit appear to be more committed to their work. In addition, according to the survey, employees who feel valued are nearly seven times more likely to recommend their organization as a good place to work.[6] The *Houston Chronicle* reported in December

Figure 4-22. Opened on Memorial Day 1930, Burbank Airport was sold to Lockheed in 1940 as World War II approached. Lockheed built the P-38 Lightning, Hudson bombers, and the B-17 bomber there during the war years, even as it continued to operate a commercial airport on site. The airport was sold back to an airport authority representing Burbank, Glendale, and Pasadena in 1978 and serves nearly 5 million people today. The visual displays that line its walls remind customers and employees of the airport's rich history.

2001 that Gen Xers, too, have a clear set of expectations of their employers and that failing to meet these expectations would reduce their commitment and increase the probability of their leaving the company.[7]

It seems as though, as much in today's environment of uncertainty as in past eras of stability, employees want to be recognized for their contributions and appreciated for what they do for their employers. This is simple common sense for many excellent leaders, yet it is often overlooked in complex organizations. In a visual management organization, one cannot ignore the employees or their contributions to the success of the organization: Employees are critical to success and deserve honor and celebration.

Lesson 4: Share Information—But Do It Carefully

In a visual management environment, an enormous amount of information is available for everyone, including management, to see. Normally, management's primary source of information is written reports and reports on the computer. However, when core leaders walk around in an open environment, they see clearly what is happening; the information is immediately available from different angles and different perspectives, and is not subject to interpretation or summarization before they see it. Moreover, the information is right there along with the work and the workers. Thus, management gets to see information in the place where the work actually occurs. Employees, too, have access to a great deal of data, which can open their eyes to a better understanding of performance needs and outcomes.

Sharing information is an important and necessary thing to do, but it should be done thoughtfully and with great care. Information must be posted in locations that employees normally pass; it must be clear and easy to follow, and it should be limited in scope. Ongoing efforts at open dialogue are crucial, in part to reinforce the message and in part to keep people focused on the changing data. Such ongoing dialogues will uncover root problems more quickly than if managers tried to figure things out for themselves.

To be truly meaningful to the employees, the information should relate directly to their jobs, and they should be able to see immediately how their efforts directly affect the metrics. Once the job performance information is linked to rewards, employees will become hooked and will become more involved than ever. In essence, everyone will now own the information.

Lesson 5: Make Results Transparent

One of the key requirements of visual management is that the link between individual and group performance must be made explicit, understandable, and obvious. In a visual management organization, everyone gets individual feedback. This feedback can come in many forms: Some organizations use formal appraisals, whereas others use periodic formal or informal feedback sessions; many develop and use individual report cards; some use 360-degree reviews; and others use comprehensive performance management systems. No matter what the type of feedback system, however, performance feedback, especially in the visual management environment, must be directly linked to rewards and recognition. In addition, this feedback must be highly visible and transparent to all.

Every person and group at every level is held accountable for and is continuously given feedback on performance. Because of this clear focus on performance, all members of the organization become vigilant about how well they are doing. With this focus, problems can be nipped in the bud, course adjustments can be made quickly, high performance can be encouraged and facilitated, and everyone knows exactly how she is doing, so there are no mysteries or surprises. This means that less energy is spent wondering what to do and more energy is devoted to the organization's core mission. Ensuring transparency of results helps ensure a focus on the required performance.

Lesson 6: Strive for Efficiency and Effectiveness

The visual management organization is designed, operated, and managed to ensure that performance results are the best they can be. Performance goals are comprehensive and have been established to improve results along two critical performance dimensions: First, the organization strives for efficiency in its operations, and second, it strives for simultaneous effectiveness. Efficiency means streamlining, moving faster, cutting out excess red tape, and making operations leaner. Getting a job done in the quickest manner possible moves it out to the customer faster and improves delivery performance. Effectiveness is all about working smarter and doing things better. Getting a job done without paying attention to the quality of the effort and the outcome wastes resources and does not fit the typical visual management culture. Working without a balance between efficiency and effectiveness, though, creates a lopsided performance outcome. Speed without quality leaves dissatisfied customers where quality counts. Conversely, too much quality can slow delivery times and also contribute to customer dissatisfaction. Hence, developing an appropriate balance between efficiency and effectiveness is crucial to successful performance in visual management organizations.

Lesson 7: Promote Innovation by Creating and Maintaining an Innovative Environment

Most organizations are perfectly designed to achieve the results they achieve. Military academies, for example, with their rigid behavior standards, strict adherence to rules, and regimented curriculum plans, have been designed to deal with problem behaviors and instill a sense of duty into their students. These academies are not typically known as hotbeds of innovation, yet they serve a particular purpose well. Heavily regulated industries, too, are not particularly innovative, since innovation cannot flourish easily in rigid, overly structured, rule-bound, static environments.

The visual management environment is not devoid of rules and structure. In fact, it has been carefully designed with clearly defined structures that support its mission. But the organization has also been designed with several core beliefs in mind: People are critical to the success of an organization and ought to be treated as if they are important, people must meet a set of clear standards and expectations set by the organization, performance must be focused on achieving the mission and goals of the organization, everyone in the organization must understand the mission and the processes that have been put in place to achieve it, and everyone has access to all of the information he needs and wants so that he can perform to the best of his ability. The visuals all work to reinforce these beliefs and to enhance the ability of employees at all levels to get the job done.

Lesson 8: Build a "Cool" Environment

A final major lesson from visual management environments is that we should remember that we are creating "cool" environments for our employees, customers, and other stakeholders. Coolness is an abstract concept with a great deal of meaning, especially to younger employees. Each of us wants a workplace in which we can take pride, one in which we want to spend time, and one that makes us feel good about spending so much time there.

A cool place is one that exudes the spirit of the times. It has images and gadgets and sounds that are exciting, stimulating, appealing, and reflective of the twenty-first century and of the work being done. Such a place challenges the mind, awakens emotions, and creates a sense of fun and importance. It is the type of place you want to show to friends and family, and the type of place in which you are proud to work.

We all know that people work more effectively in clean, well-lit, uncluttered, well-organized workspaces, and there are lots of those in many different kinds of organizations. But these workspaces are not necessarily inspirational or instructional or cool. They do not always reflect the collective energy, vitality, and creativity of a visual management environment. Employees feel more connected to visual management organizations than to more traditional ones; they enjoy showing the space off to visitors, and they often bring family members and friends in to see what is going on. They appreciate the effort it takes to create one of these spaces, they know from comparisons that their workplace has achieved something special, and they are excited to be a part of it. This enthusiasm translates into performance every time.

CHAPTER 5

Road Map to Visual Management—Planning and Preparation

At this point, you have become familiar with the background of visual management, you understand the foundations supporting this concept, and you have learned what a visual management organization looks like. It is now time to learn how to create a plan for becoming a visual management organization. This chapter and the next provide a road map to guide you through preparation for and achievement of the six phases of visual management planning and implementation. They help you understand what you should do at each step, how to do it, and why you should take that step. Finally, they explain the benefits and expected outcomes of each phase of the visual management process.

As you begin to think about implementing visual management, keep in mind that it utilizes a holistic approach to organization and performance improvement. It relies on the strength of the system design and the competence of the leaders to bring an organization, a company, or a department to a new and higher, more sustainable level of performance. Results are seen very quickly, although this is not an overnight success story. Significant planning, which is the focus of this chapter, and careful attention to implementation, which is the focus of Chapter 6, are necessary to ensure the successful adoption of visual management, although it may take on a life of its own as it spreads through the organization. Visual management rapidly becomes a way of life, keeping people engaged in and excited by organizational results.

■ Getting Ready for Visual Management

During the six phases of the visual management implementation process, you will review and, if necessary, revise the core elements of the design of your organization: the structural system, including the physical plant; the technical systems, including work flow and processes; and the decision-making and information-sharing processes, including systems for managing recognition, rewards, feedback, involvement, accountability, and performance. This review is critical to ensure that the best systems for achieving an organization's central purpose have been developed and that these management systems are aligned so that they work in concert with one another.

With particular regard to performance, a solid review of key performance indicators, which are the critical performance metrics for the unit, must be conducted to ensure that there are no surprises for anyone in the organization. These performance expectations and metrics must be consistent with the organization's mission, vision, and stated goals, and all managers and employees must know and understand these key indicators. Everyone in the organization must become familiar with everything that is expected of anyone in the organization or unit so that all the people can see how their efforts fit into and affect overall performance.

Reward systems are reviewed to ensure that they are linked directly to clear performance goals. It is also important to make sure that people receive adequate training to help them succeed in the new environment that is being created. People will need to understand visual management, as well as the requirements of the system. The ultimate success of visual management relies on careful preparation and solid planning and assessment activities.

Champions and Change Agents

The adoption of visual management is a change process in an organization, and it will not work without appropriate attention and support. Like most change efforts, it requires change agents or champions within the adopting organization to lead the effort. Typically, change agents and champions are the leaders of the organization that is undergoing the change, whether that organization is a company, a division, a team, or a department. Usually there is one clear champion who develops a vision of what the organization might be and carries the message into the organization. Occasionally there is more than one champion, and a change agent team emerges. These change agents should be core members of the visual management team.

The typical champion is an individual who has been exposed to visual management through a presentation, through discussion with other leaders or managers, by visiting a visual management organization, or by having read this book or an article about the process. After this initial exposure, the champion has continued to seek out more details about visual management and its implementation from other adopters and from written material. Leaders in visual management organizations often spend a fair amount of time with potential change agents and champions from other organizations, helping them fully grasp the visual management concept to take back to their own organizations. Regardless of how the champion or change agent learned about the concept, though, he has gathered enough information about it to recognize that it can make an enormous difference in his organization.

Once a leader has discovered visual management, she often spends time acquainting others with the concepts and gaining further support for an implementation. This is an important preliminary step in any change process: Few organizations manage successful change without support from their leaders. Visual management, though, creates excitement quickly because of its power. Corporate visitors to the VA Regional Office, for example, are stunned as they tour the facility. As they speak with employees, they can see and feel the impact that visual management has had on the place, and they know that they want to take it home with them to improve their own organizations. Many request second and third visits and become stalwart converts to visual management. These people often spread the word with a zeal that can seem evangelical to some, yet their enthusiasm and energy are critical to the successful implementation of such a system. Columbus Regional Hospital often has a similar impact, and visitors from around the world have come there to learn more about this remarkable environment and the use of visual arts in its healing mission.

The Visual Management Team

Once an organization has decided to adopt visual management, it is imperative that it identify a visual management team to spearhead the effort. This team will be responsible for initiating the visual management activities, leading the educational and assimilation efforts, and maintaining the focus and direction of the process. The members of this team may change over time as more and more people in the organization become excited about visual management, although the initial champions usually remain as team members, as their contributions may be critical for continuity. The visual management team is usually made up of eight to ten individuals who are committed to the concept; they should represent the organization's leaders, the workforce, the union, where one exists, and the organization's other stakeholders as much as possible. Of course, the number may vary somewhat depending on the size and complexity of the organization.

In addition to being representative of the organization, members of the team should have the full range of critical knowledge, skills, and abilities (KSAs) required to implement visual management. If other knowledge, skills, and abilities are needed, the team should have access to them on an ad hoc basis. The team must also have access to resources for implementing visual management. Critical KSAs for the visual management team include a full understanding of the organization's work processes, a full comprehension of the metrics and how they relate to one another, an ability to understand the perspective of both the customer and the workforce, and some expertise in organizational systems design and human resource management. They will also need some understanding of interior design, space management, and construction, and some degree of knowledge and skill in both the fine arts and graphic arts. In addition, the team should have sufficient institutional memory to understand the current dynamics of the organization and their roots in history.

These KSAs are important to the effort for a variety of reasons. Clearly, knowledge of the work processes is crucial, since any changes that affect people and how they work may have an impact on these processes. The visual management team must know where change or movement is possible and where it is not. They must understand the financial and work-flow implications of what they want to do, and they must be able to determine where improvements in work flow are needed and where they are not. Without clear knowledge of work processes, there is not a true understanding of the organization or of the systems required to make it operate effectively.

There is also a need for sufficient institutional memory to ensure that the team builds upon what is important to the organization and lets go of what is not important. Knowledge of the organization's culture, history, systems, people, and purpose provides a sense of the organization's evolution, of why and how it became what it is today. Armed with this information, the team can develop a solid feel for the organization's dynamics, can ground its activities and plans in the reality of the organization, and can ensure consistency in the links between past and future.

Clearly, this team needs to have or to develop a full comprehension of the metrics and how they relate to one another. One of the critical tasks of visual management is to make performance results highly visible and crystal clear. In order to have a positive impact on performance outcomes, however, these results must be appropriate to the unit to which they are linked, must be identifiable for accountability, and must be important to the success of the unit. Consider, for example, an organization that espouses quality as its most important outcome, but measures only quantity of output. If the output results reported visually show only quantity produced, then this visual cue tells employees that quantity is crucial and quality is not even on the radar screen. The team must know the metrics in order to ensure that the visual cues send the right messages.

A successful visual management team will also be able to understand the perspectives of both the customer and the workforce. Despite concerted efforts on the part of organizations in general over the last ten years or so to ensure a clear customer focus, many organizations have not succeeded in putting a real face on the customer for their employees. Visual management does this clearly and in a highly visible manner; hence, the team will need to understand the customer in order to do the best work possible in its customer focus activities. The same is true of employees, who are celebrated in a visual management organization. The team will need to learn what is important to employees so that it knows what to celebrate and how best to do that. In addition, in a union environment, the team must have an understanding of the union and its history in the organization. Unions are part of the personality of an organization: They have vital contributions to make, and they must be included in visual management efforts and celebrated as an important part of the organizational context.

Certainly, some expertise in organization design, systems alignment, and human resource management is important to this process. Team members need enough knowledge to understand the concepts and desired outcomes of system alignment as well as the ramifications of various changes for human resource policies. They also need to understand the regulatory environment and any contractual obligations to ensure that the design they produce is in concert with these. The visual management team will be leading efforts to improve organizational performance. Sometimes this means changing systems and design elements; other times it requires reorganization of people and processes. A team with solid knowledge of these elements has a much higher likelihood of success in the implementation process.

Although most organizations, with some very obvious exceptions, do not hire employees with the expectation that they will be great artists, architects, or interior designers, some understanding of space management, construction, and interior design will be helpful on the team. Visual management, after all, does suggest some changes in physical space beyond hanging art on the walls. Having some expertise in these areas will help the team to work toward an integrated and comprehensive physical design.

Employees in many organizations have hidden artistic talent and skills. It is helpful if one or more of these people are included in the visual management team. Because of their training and interest in fine arts and graphic arts, they can help in translating good ideas into visual cues for the team and the organization. Not everyone on the team need be an artist, but having one or two is very helpful. At a minimum, someone with an unusually good eye for color and design is necessary to the team.

One Leader/One Vision

It is important to note that, while the team as a whole will be responsible for implementing visual management in the organization, it is absolutely necessary for this team to have a leader. Visual management can be designed by a team or a group with appropriate facilitation and direction, but the implementation cannot be well managed by an uncoordinated committee. Implementation must be led by a champion who has the authority, the vision, and the power to make change happen. To film a motion picture, for example, requires hundreds, if not thousands, of people. However, it also requires one vision, which is typically that of the director. Without this, the film will be disjointed and uneven. The same concept applies to visual management: *There must be one vision.* The visual management champion must have the ability to look into the future and see how the visuals will fit together in three to five years and must be flexible enough to adjust to changing situations along the way.

This vision does not have to be one person's vision; it can be the joint vision of the organization or of a leadership group within the organization. This is, in fact, preferable, and we encourage organizations to include as wide a group as possible in developing the vision in order to gain commitment early in the process. At a minimum, the vision must represent the beliefs of both the champion and the visual management team, once they have considered the beliefs of the organization and its other members. A single vision is an absolute necessity for the success of visual management. Visual management focuses stakeholders on a particular mission, and the actual work in the organization is supposed to focus on the accomplishment of that mission. Having and supporting a single vision helps to avoid situations in which lots of different people begin making decisions out of context that don't relate to one another.

Team Start-Up Activities

Once the visual management team has been selected, it must be prepared for its tasks. Initial preparation involves an introduction to the principles and practice of visual management, visits to one or more visual management sites, and the initiation of team-building efforts directed at defining norms and expectations for the team. Roles and responsibilities must be determined, and the team must also establish performance goals and metrics to provide feedback on how well it is doing. Access to some of the resources targeted for the visual management process is helpful, and the team should make arrangements to understand the initial resource commitment. It is important for this team to define communication methods, time lines, and patterns for informing the organization about its activities. If the team works too much behind closed doors, it runs a high risk of becoming isolated from the organization, and the visual management process will suffer. One key goal in preparing for the implementation of visual management is to develop a solid team with an effective leader to spearhead the effort. This makes all the difference in the success of the transition to visual management.

A good initial project for this team is to create a record of how the organization looks before the change effort begins. During this step, the team can test its norms and values, iron out any weaknesses, and build a sense of cohesion and camaraderie. The point of getting a baseline at the initial start-up is to ensure that stakeholders in the organization will be able to see how far they have come as the process progresses. Consider how weight loss companies take photographs of their clients before, during, and after their weight loss. These photographs inspire the clients, individually and as a group, to continue with the program; they celebrate the program's success stories; and they are great advertisements for other people who are thinking about joining the program. An organization that is converting to visual management should do the same thing, and this is a perfect start-up activity for the visual management team. Before and after photos, like those shown in Figures 5-1 and 5-2, can be simply astounding in the improvements they show. They can also reinforce the positive aspects of the changes by helping people focus on the progress they have made along the way.

Too often, great change processes are not well documented, and the lessons learned at each step of the way are lost. In visual management, it is particularly important to capture the before and after images because of the impact of the visual changes. Photographs and videos of the organization taken before, during, and after the transformation provide a comprehensive record of the physical changes. These records are of great value to the organization as it celebrates its successes and announces to the world how much it has improved.

Figure 5-1. How would you like to work in this space? The clutter, low lighting, mismatched furniture, and general disorder make it an uncomfortable and disorganized workplace.

It is also good to have a record of the thoughts and planning sessions that occur during the visual management process. Graphic facilitation of meetings begins to acquaint people with the visual components and cues that they will learn to rely on in a visual management environment. This process utilizes drawings combined with key words, as shown in the graphic in Figure 5-3, to enable the team to capture visually the structure and scope of its subject, the relationships of the key points, and the relative importance of these key points. It also allows the group to step back, examine the total picture of its thoughts, and see how all of its ideas fit together. Graphic processes such as this are a perfect fit with visual management systems: They can be used effectively to capture the spirit of ongoing planning and implementation, and they are visual in nature and hence reinforce the process itself.

Figure 5-2. This is the same workplace as in Figure 5-1 after implementing visual management. The clutter is gone, the space is organized and bright, and the mission is clear.

■ A Six-Phase Process

An organization that is considering the adoption of visual management should think of the development and implementation process as having six phases: plan, frame, create, focus, detail, and renew. Briefly, phase 1 is a planning process in which we clarify the mission, vision, and goals of the organization. Phase 2 is a framing process in which we review and revise organizational systems and structures. These two phases are covered in detail in this chapter. As Chapter 6 explains, phase 3 is devoted to the initial creation of the new physical space and its visual attributes, phase 4 focuses on the customer and the history of the organization, phase 5 is a fine-tuning stage, and

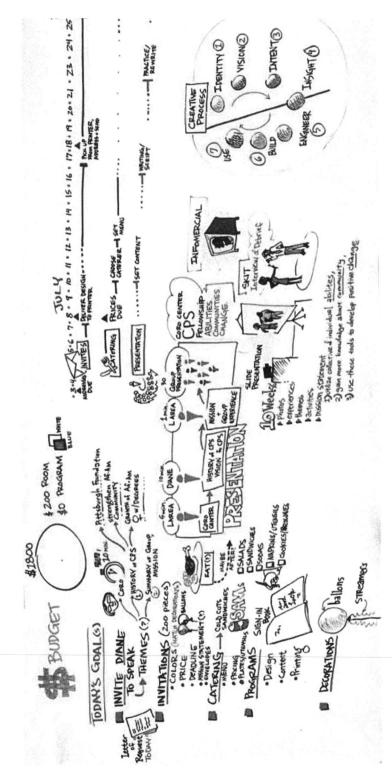

Figure 5-3. Graphic facilitation is a way of facilitating groups using a visual shorthand to track and frame the discussion on large murals. As this example shows, the graphics that are integrated into the chart replace many words and stimulate more creative thinking about the topic at hand. (Drawing by Peter Durand, Alphachimp Studios.)

phase 6 is an important renewal phase. Hence, this chapter focuses on the assessment and foundation-building requirements of visual management, and Chapter 6 focuses on the physical and performance changes that are visual management's core elements.

In these two chapters, we have listed and described each visual management phase as a distinct step in the process, and we have separated preparation from action. The reality, though, is that the phases often blend together, and the distinctions among them may blur. In fact, depending upon the situation, certain decisions that are required in one phase may have to be made in an earlier or later phase of the process, and sometimes organizations engage in several phases in parallel, rather than sequentially.

In addition, if an organization is unusually strong in one section and weak in another, it may need to work through these phases in an order other than the one that is implied. For example, in the last two decades, many organizations have put a great deal of effort into developing better knowledge of their customers and improving customer relations. If a particular organization has not put a similar level of effort into improving its performance management systems, it may need to work first on the detailing of phase 5 rather than the focusing of phase 4; or an organization may find that some of its early preparation work in phase 2 is inconsistent with its later work in phase 4 or 5, and so it may need to make adjustments. Thus, although the description of visual management implementation in these chapters is strictly sequential, it is important to understand that both the process and the approach can and should be tailored to the particular circumstances of the adopting organization. Flexibility and adaptability are important for the effective planning and implementation of visual management.

As we begin to consider preparing an organization for visual management, it is helpful to start with an overview of the entire process. Figure 5-4 provides this overview graphically. This road map representation gives us a quick visual reference to the various phases, stages, and steps in the process and can be helpful in reminding us

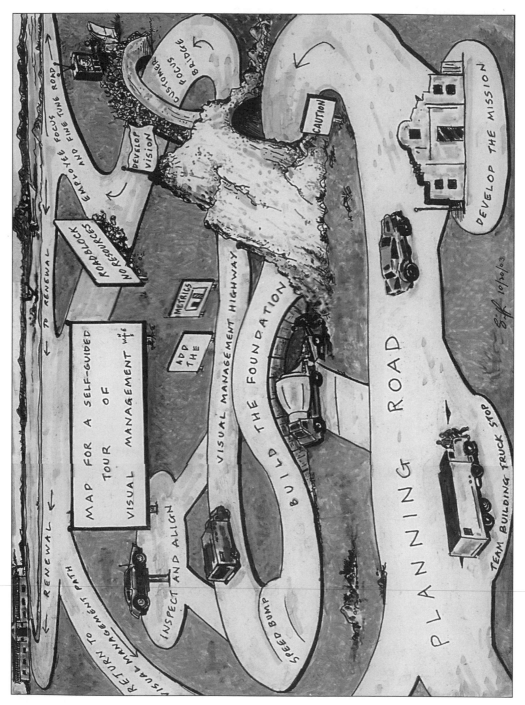

Figure 5-4. The visual management road map provides an overview of the entire process and serves as a visual point of reference for planning, development, and implementation.

where we are at any given point in time and what will be expected next. The current chapter focuses primarily on the activities shown in the lower half of the road map–planning and building a foundation.

Phase 1: Planning

Every new plan or process within an organization needs a clear starting point. With visual management, that starting point is the development and refinement of the mission, vision, and core values of the organization. It is crucial that we clarify and understand the organization's goals and priorities, since these become the guides for all of our efforts. All activities in this phase of the visual management process are aimed at developing a written and visual plan that sketches out how the organization will look three to five years down the road. In essence, this is the phase in which a true vision of the organization's future is created, and organization members come to have a sense of ownership of that future vision.

Concurrent with the development of the mission, vision, and core values, the concept of visual management must be introduced to key players in the organization, including, but not limited to, all managers, supervisors, union leaders, and other key constituents. Key players must understand and accept the rationale for implementing visual management and must know how visual management will contribute to the achievement of the organization's mission, vision, and core values. A clear overview of visual management is critical at this point, since this will provide a framework for understanding how the mission, vision, and core values will be communicated and implemented within the organization. This overview will also help foster critical thinking about the concept of visual management and ensure that a multitude of midcourse corrections will not be required at some future point because someone did not understand the goals of visual management or the direction it was taking. This is also an appropriate time at which to develop a communication plan for the rest of the organization to ensure that all employees will know what visual management is about and why it is being adopted.

It is important at this point to reemphasize that the critical starting point for the implementation of a visual management plan is for all members of the organization, especially the visual management team, to become very clear about the organization's mission, vision, and core values. It is also necessary to link the mission, vision, and core values to explicit organizational goals. Without a clear and specific understanding of what the organization is about and where it plans to go, visual management cannot live up to its highest potential.

Many companies have spent some time and effort on clarifying who and what they are. This typically culminates in some form of explicit statement of the company's mission; it often also results in the development of a vision statement that encompasses a statement of core values and guiding principles for the organization, and this statement is sometimes linked to the overarching goals of the company. In the visual management environment, attention must be paid to all three of these issues.

An organization needs a clear and well-defined mission that explicitly signals to employees, customers, and others why the organization exists and what it expects to achieve. For example, Columbus Regional Hospital (CRH) in Columbus, Indiana, evolved from a small county hospital into a regional referral center and has always been known for high-quality, compassionate care. Its mission is: "Improve the health and well-being of the people we serve." According to CRH's 2003–2004 strategic plan, the hospital aims to accomplish this mission through the achievement of four critical performance goals: employee and patient satisfaction, financial results, quality and safety, and growth and innovation. From this, it is clear that employee and patient satisfaction and excellent service are crucial goals, in addition to the more typical business goals of cost, quality, and delivery. The mission is straightforward and clear, and the hospital's motto, "Miles Ahead. Not Miles Away," is also consistent with its mission and goals.

A vision statement helps to clarify the mission by defining how the mission will be achieved: It incorporates the core values into a statement of how the organization and its people will act to carry out the mission. CRH has crafted a powerful vision statement: "Columbus Regional Hospital and its Medical Staff will lead the development of the healthcare delivery system of choice for those we serve." This is more fully explained in a booklet designed for distribution to the broad community that describes what it means to CRH to be a regional hospital. The CRH vision of excellence defines a regional hospital as one that is committed to advanced technology, high-quality safe care, and extraordinary service; it also means having outstanding doctors and being nationally recognized for outstanding work by doctors, employees, and volunteers.[1] This hospital has taken great care to ensure that all stakeholders understand its commitment to excellence and has incorporated its core values into its mission and vision.

For any organization, the core values make a statement of what the organization stands for and how its people will act in order to achieve its goals. Another example of an organization in which the statement of core values is detailed and clear is UltraViolet Devices, Inc. This company's statement of core values is straightforward: "UVDI focuses energy and resources toward being a customer driven, high quality product manufacturer. We achieve this goal through insistence on total quality communication, significant training commitment for organizational team development, and management's fundamental belief in basic core leadership principles and values."[2] Three further paragraphs in the core values statement provide details about UVDI's commitment to developing and nurturing win-win relationships among employees, customers, and suppliers; about the most appropriate communication model for the organization; and about what quality really means there. There is little room for misinterpretation of what this company considers critical in terms of its mission, vision, and core values.

Another example shows this in another light. Some years ago, on a ride from Jacksonville Airport to the elegant and award-winning Ritz-Carlton Hotel in Amelia Island, Florida, the hotel's chauffeur offered his business card, saying that he and all members of the Ritz-

Carlton staff would be happy to do anything they could to make this visit a memorable one. Printed on the back of the card was the Ritz-Carlton motto, which captured beautifully a sense of the core values of the hotel and resort: "We are ladies and gentlemen serving ladies and gentlemen." A core values statement may be as short and succinct as this, or it may be a page or two in length; it may be a list, a series of visual images, carefully written prose, or a combination of these. To be effective, however, it must reflect the true character of what the organization expects from its employees, what it gives back to its employees and other stakeholders, and the values for which it will hold employees accountable. HP Financial Services (HPFS) focused directly on important core values when it posted the sign shown in Figure 5-5. It makes a simple, clear, and powerful statement about what is important to this group in order to achieve success.

Creating Mission, Vision, and Core Values Statements

Many people in organizations today believe that they know all about mission, vision, and core values. After all, they have sat in meetings discussing these issues or participated in groups charged with developing them. The truth of the matter, though, is that it is much easier to talk about these concepts than to capture them in concrete terms or clarify them so that they become the key behavioral and performance guidelines for the organization. The process of creating clear and useful statements of mission, vision, and core values begins with the selection of a group of key leaders, stakeholders, and employees who will serve as the core group to clarify what the organization's mission, vision, and goals really are. Although the visual management team can do this, it is usually better to get a broader representative sample of the people in the organization involved. Outside stakeholders are also sometimes included in this process. Leadership is crucial to the success of this group, as is good facilitation. A facilitator is usually needed to keep the group focused, engaged, and on point.

As a group, this team must answer a series of questions for the organization, then collate the responses and produce a coherent and

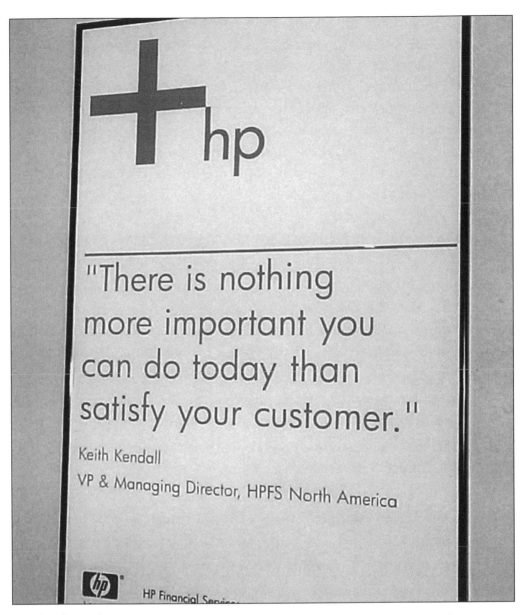

Figure 5-5. Impressive in size, vibrantly colored, and hanging in the most trafficked areas at HP Financial Services headquarters in Murray Hill, New Jersey, motivational posters about HPFS's passion for customers are constant reminders that the number one priority here is improving the total customer experience.

compelling statement of mission, vision, and core values. The process starts with a commitment to identifying where the organization is going and where it is expected to be in three to five years. Next, the team must gather information about the organization. This information-gathering step is similar to an environmental scan, which is often undertaken in organizational change processes and search conference methodologies.[3] The following questions provide a starting point for the group and should be considered carefully, as they will inform the final statements:

❑ What is our core mission? Has it changed over time? Does it need to change? What are the implications of any such changes for our core businesses?

❑ What do we know about our business direction? Where have we been going? How are we doing? How are our competitors doing? Are we doing what we need and want to be doing? Do we need to consider changing the way we do business?

❑ Are we participating in appropriate markets? Are our business units relevant in today's business environment?

❑ Who are our customers? Who are our suppliers? What do they think of us? How do we treat them?

❑ Who are our other important stakeholders? How do we deal with them? How do they deal with us? Do our expectations match?

❑ How do our employees feel? How are they treated? What can we learn about their attitudes and behaviors?

❑ What kind of changes and challenges are ahead of us? Will we need new skills and knowledge down the road? What will be the impact of changing technology on our people and our business?

❑ What do we believe in? Do we all embrace the same values? Have our values changed over time? Do they need to change?

Collection and collation of the data gathered in this step is important for the creation or refinement of the needed mission, vision, and core values statements. The data provide a clear and comprehensive overview of organizational attributes and the beliefs of the stakeholders. These must be incorporated into the statements that will guide the organization into the future.

Assessment of Readiness for Visual Management

Once the initial questions about the business, the values, and the people have been asked, and once the information needed to develop a clear picture of the organization and its mission has been gathered, the group must assess the value that could be added by visual management and the degree of organizational commitment to it. The pattern of questions that must be answered at this point helps produce a readiness assessment for the organization:

❑ Is visual management right for this organization? Do we want to have a culture that is highly focused on the mission and the customer?

❑ Are we willing to share full information with our employees?

❑ How will our organization react to visual management? Will our management team support such an approach? Will our employees embrace it? Can we help them do this? Are we willing and able to make the necessary investments?

❑ Do our key leaders fully support visual management? Do they understand the investment in time, energy, and resources that will be required if we are to enable the organization to achieve its full visual management potential? Are the leaders in this for the long haul? Are they prepared to continually support this program until it becomes fully ingrained in the organization?

❑ Do we have management support for the process? Does management truly understand the concept of visual management and the principles behind it? If not, are we prepared to teach this to management?

❑ Are the right managers in place to support the concept? Are we prepared to educate, coach, or even change some managers if necessary?

❑ Do the supervisors understand and support visual management? Do they see its value? Are they willing and able to convince the employees of its value? Do they understand the organization's metrics? Are they prepared to track and post those metrics and explain them to the employees?

After this set of questions has been answered and the responses have been analyzed, it is time to begin to address concerns and issues that surface during this analysis of results. For example, if there appears to be insufficient understanding of visual management among the employees, the visual management team will need to develop a strategy for better communication and education about the process and its anticipated results.

Particular attention should be paid to middle managers and supervisors in this planning phase. These are the people who will have the most impact on the implementation effort in the organization. If they do not understand and commit to visual management, the implementation process may stumble. The organization must make sure that it has the right middle managers and supervisors in key positions for the implementation process. Those who support visual management will make it happen in their areas, those who are willing to learn about it will learn to make it happen, and those who have already demonstrated some flexibility and openness to change will be able to grow to support it. Keep in mind, however, that those middle managers and supervisors who are skeptical of or even opposed to visual management and organizational change can also play a valuable role in the implementation process. Cynics and resistors often point out potential hurdles to adoption and thus can, if their observations are channeled appropriately, be of great help. It is important to listen to this group, but also to ensure that it does not have the power to undermine the effort.

When the organization is clear about its mission, vision, and guiding principles and has put the right leaders in place, the stage has been set for further efforts. At this point, all key players are involved in the process, the organization has a clear direction, the leaders have a broad understanding of the design principles of organizational systems and can begin to influence others, and the path to follow for making visual management real is emerging.

Creating a Visual Road Map

The final step in phase 1 is the creation of a visual road map that encompasses the mission, vision, and core values and broadly lays out for everyone how the organization will achieve its mission. This road map can be a drawing, a picture, or a computer-generated image that captures for the organization and for the stakeholders what the organization is about, where the organization is going, why it is going there, and how it will get there. In Chapter 4, Figure 4-11 shows an actual organizational road map that was used by the Department of Veterans Affairs to guide implementation of visual management at one of its regional offices.

Once the road map has been completed, it should be broadcast widely throughout the organization. Large copies can be posted at strategic viewing points in the facility, and smaller copies should be distributed to all employees and key stakeholders. This road map will send a definite message that things in the organization are changing, and it often will generate real excitement about the mission and the role that visual management can play in its accomplishment. Organizations are often surprised at how many employees post the road map in their workspace, yet they should recognize that this is the first stage at which people begin to see the power of visual images.

By the end of the first phase of visual management implementation, a number of requirements have been satisfied. First, the visual management implementation team has been established and has successfully completed some tasks that are absolutely necessary to the continuing success of the implementation. Second, this planning phase has helped ensure that a wide acknowledgment and broad understanding of visual management exists in the organization. Third, the process has helped to build confidence in the system among the organization's leaders; middle managers and supervisors know that they must help lead and support the effort, and the organization has ensured that those who are in key positions to influence the process have the capacity to grow with it. The first phase of implementation has also provided appropriate individuals with an in-depth understanding of visual management so that they can continue to spearhead the effort. Finally, the organization has developed a mission, vision, and core values statement to help guide it through the process, and a visual road map has been created to show everyone the intended path to success.

Phase 2: Building a Framework

Phase 2 focuses on ensuring that the organization has the appropriate structures and systems to carry out its mission properly. At this point, the organization really begins to prepare for change. The visual management team and other key players learn about assessing and redesigning the organization's systems in order to ensure the alignment necessary for effective performance, and they begin the assessment and design processes.

The initial education effort of this phase has several learning goals. First, the team needs to understand clearly that visual management is a powerful set of tools to enhance organizational performance, but that it is not a stand-alone process. They will need to understand how different organizational systems and frameworks fit together and how they are designed to influence the behaviors, feelings, and attributes of the employees. Systems and guiding frameworks are those elements that are designed to make an organization work effectively. They include the management structure, operating systems, human resource systems and policies, technical systems, decision-making processes, and information-sharing and communication systems.

The team also needs to understand that visual management is used in concert with a clear organizational model that focuses on aligning organizational systems for performance improvement. The team members need to know why visual management is being adopted and what the anticipated outcomes will be, and to support this. They also need to appreciate the basic principles of fine arts, especially color and design, and the power of images in today's environment. Furthermore, they must understand the way in which the world is becoming more visual and why organizations are turning to the power of visuals to improve performance.

In essence, the organization is being prepared for change, and it is becoming very clear to all the organization's stakeholders that visual management is an enhancement to all of the traditional management systems. An organization in which people can see the synergies among their systems is one in which people understand how the various pieces should fit together. The more they understand that these pieces can be carefully designed to fit together, the more they will see that there is a single broad goal in a visual management implementation. That goal is performance improvement.

Education and Design

Usually, phase 2 encompasses both educational and action components for a broader segment of the organization. The educational phase combines personal with group learning. After some initial reading to familiarize participants with visual management concepts and the basics of organization design, presentations are made by visual management experts and by representatives of companies that have adopted the visual management philosophy and use the visual management tools and techniques at their sites. If possible, visits to one of these visual management sites by the organization's leaders, the members of the visual management team, and other key players will further increase their enthusiasm for the approach. A series of seminars, training sessions, and other learning opportunities is typically offered to bring the visual management team and other relevant stakeholders to a new level of understanding about the design of effective organizations and their operating systems. In addition, the visual management team will engage in data-gathering and assessment activities, as well as action planning for some early physical changes in the organization.

The educational activities focus on helping the organization's stakeholders build synergy among important systems. At the core of good organization design is the alignment of organizational systems to best achieve the mission of the unit, but alignment usually does not happen by accident. Deliberate efforts must be made to align the organization's mission, vision, values, goals, and strategies with the capabilities of the people and the technical and support systems in order to achieve the desired performance improvements. Developing tactics and strategies for creating and enhancing this alignment is an important element of the educational aspect of phase 2 in visual management.

Most organizations have some familiarity with the concepts of organization design based upon their own earlier change efforts, or upon the efforts of other organizations. It is important to the success of visual management that the design of the organization be analyzed for appropriate system alignment. As Chapter 3 clearly explained, there are a variety of system design models and processes from which to select the one that best fits philosophically and practically with the organization. We encourage the use of models based on the values and principles of sociotechnical systems theory because they work toward achieving a balance between the people and the technology and processes of the organization. However, as long as the design methodology is focused on system alignment, it will work well with visual management.

Once a model of organization design and system alignment and a process for assessing this have been selected, the visual management team should lead a review and assessment effort to determine whether the organization is well designed, whether the design needs tweaking, or whether a major redesign is in order. The team must review people, processes, and technology systems to ensure that they work in concert with one another.

The review of people systems focuses on how people are treated in the organization, what human resource policies and procedures are in place, the level and quality of training that is available and required, the degree of people's involvement in and accountability for their decisions and actions, and performance management systems and procedures. There is little doubt that feedback systems have an impact on performance, and in phase 2 it is important to assess this link directly by answering the following questions:

❑ Are people getting timely and appropriate feedback on their actions and performance?

❑ Does the feedback system focus on getting the right information to the right people? Is the system timely, accurate, and well directed?

Recognition and reward systems, too, are important connectors between behavior and performance outcomes. The review of these human resource systems should show whether there is a clear link between actual and desired behavior and performance outcomes, and how well the reward and recognition systems support this link.

Also critically important is careful analysis of the performance management system. In many organizations, this system has become misaligned and even dysfunctional. A good performance management system ensures that employees throughout the organization know what is expected of them, that they get consistent and timely feedback on how well they are performing relative to expectations, and that the outcomes of their efforts are dealt with appropriately. It also provides employees with assistance in improving. The system must focus employees' attention on the mission and goals of the organization and keep them on track so that they can work toward achieving those goals.

In addition to the people systems that must be analyzed, there are several decision-making and information-management elements that must be aligned if the organization is to be successful. These processes are important to the successful achievement of the organization's mission and goals: A clear decision-making structure is needed to ensure that good decisions are made, and strong communication systems and processes are crucial for effective information management. Knowledge of who will make what decisions, and at what level, is a starting point for a solid decision-making system. In addition to this, it is important to clarify a process for decision making or a set of processes for different types of decisions. Finally, it is important to identify appropriate information dissemination channels so that the decisions that have been made are communicated to those who will be affected by them. This systematic review ensures that the organization has developed or refined its communication, decision-making, and operating systems so that they support the mission and the employees who must carry out that mission.

Reassessment of organizational processes is important to ensure that proper procedures are in place to accomplish the mission. This typically involves a brief analysis of practices related to all aspects of the work flow, including task assignments, position descriptions, and relative responsibilities. The goal of this review is to avoid redundancies and duplications of effort and to ensure that quality is built into the system so that the organization can perform as efficiently and effectively as possible.

In a review of technology, the team should look at the choices that have been made regarding the equipment and its functions. It should assess whether the right technology is in place, whether that technology is flexible enough to grow as needs change, whether it is proprietary or off-the-shelf, and whether it will support the long-range needs of the organization. With the continued emphasis on productivity improvement, the manner in which technology is used is becoming increasingly important. If any of these choices are misaligned, this could have a significant impact on the organization's short- and long-term performance.

Physical Audit and Assessment

In this second phase of visual management, we also begin to assess the physical space to determine whether our overall physical themes, such as color and lighting, fit where we need to go and whether they will support the dramatic changes that will be made down the road. Stand in the center of a workspace in your organization and slowly turn in a full circle, looking at everything around you, as you ask yourself the following questions:

❏ What do you see? What colors stand out? Are there many colors, or is there a basic color scheme?

❏ What do you see on the walls, ceilings, and floors? What do the equipment and/or furniture look like?

❏ Do you have a sense of coherence and cohesiveness? Or do you see a mixed bag of colors, styles, and décor?

During the physical audit that is initiated in this phase, questions such as these will help guide your assessment. For example, take a look at the color scheme in the area in which you are working:

❏ Is there a deliberate color scheme that fits together and unifies the space visually, or are there random colors that give a sense of disjointedness?

❏ What do the colors that are in place say about this space and this organization?

❏ If there is coherence in the color scheme, does it fit the organization? Will it fit over the long term?

It would probably not, for example, make much sense to plan a color scheme based on blues and purples for a John Deere parts manufacturing facility or distribution center, since green is so widely associated with the company. As the color scheme is assessed, it is important to remember to include the walls, the ceilings, the carpets, the file cabinets, the partitions, the furniture, and other items in the space. The ultimate goal of this assessment of the color scheme is to ensure that these elements work in concert and fit the organization, yet are simple enough to accommodate and support the vast number of visuals that will be added later.

In the visual management organization, well-displayed, powerful images almost always trigger positive feedback. Over time, as more visuals are added to the workspaces, there will be a tendency to want to add even more. This could lead to a situation in which there is a series of impressive displays that don't fit together, and this leads to mixed messages and a diffusion of the power of the visual displays. The fit is critical in visual management: It is this cohesion, or fit, that keeps people focused on a single vision and the organization's mission and goals. Developing lots of great visual images is not the point of visual management; the real reason to adopt visual management is its power in focusing employees on the right goals through the use of coordinated visual displays.

Another area on which to focus attention during the physical audit is the lighting in the facility. Lighting is often a neglected part of organization design, and many organizations have insufficient lighting for employees to work effectively. One of the most basic tenets of visual management is to make sure that the workspace is not underlit, causing physical discomfort, eyestrain, or anything along those lines. If a workspace is underlit, this will weaken the power of the visuals to be added later. Imagine an art gallery or museum that displayed works of art without adequate lighting.

When the lighting audit is performed, it is also important, and an appropriate time, to look at the ergonomics of the situation. Just as the lighting audit focuses on how well people can perform their work under current lighting conditions, the ergonomics audit helps to ensure that people are not injuring themselves, winding up with carpal tunnel syndrome or other maladies that reduce their ability to perform.

One plant manager in a large printing company made significant improvements in productivity by investing in new paint and lights on the manufacturing floor. Little had been done to change this facility for nearly twenty years before he came on board, and press operators running large orders on complex presses had become accustomed to working in dim light. The change to a bright blue and white color scheme, combined with bright and well-directed lighting, had a significant and immediate positive effect on the error rate in the facility.

When the lighting assessment is conducted, it is important to watch people working and address the following issues:

❑ Is there adequate light in the primary work areas? Is there any natural light that can be better accessed?

❑ Is the artificial light bright enough, or does it produce a blinding glare? Does the light add a sense of cheer, or is it sterile and unappealing?

❑ Does the lighting support and enhance the space for the addition of future visuals, or will it merely cloak them in darkness?

Improving the lighting and paying attention to ergonomics can have an enormous impact on productivity, but keep in mind that visual management is much more than simply an emphasis on lighting. In short, we need to think about the lighting as a design element that is a piece of the structural system that supports the mission, vision, and core values. All of the design elements should fit together as part of this structural system, just as the structural systems should fit together as part of the broader management systems.

Another area requiring attention in the physical audit is the physical clutter and chaos that exists in most organizations. Clutter, as well as being unsightly, gets in the way of efficient and effective work, and when there is a lot of chaos and personal clutter, it is very difficult to build a cohesive, coherent visual design for the organization. As an organization moves into the visual management paradigm, removing clutter and beginning to build a framework of neatness sets the stage for the later phases. Of course, it also sends a message that clutter is unacceptable and counterproductive, and it supports potential core values such as professionalism and efficiency.

At this point, it is also important to begin thinking about core themes for the visual displays. For example, a hospital might want to focus on medicine, research, and stories about how it helped the community, whereas a manufacturing plant could focus on the manufacturing process, its products, and how those products have met customers' needs. The number and variety of themes that an organization chooses will vary greatly depending upon the organization's mission, strategies, complexity, and markets, although the best choice is to err on the side of simplicity and organize the displays around a few broad themes, thus ensuring a sense of organization and continuity. Figures 5-6 and 5-7 show one lobby display at the Municipal Securities Rulemaking Board (MSRB); it reflects the board's mission, relates its history, and works to enhance its corporate identity.

As early as the start of phase 2 of the visual management process, the organization should be beginning to put the necessary pieces in place so that in later phases they will all fit together. In fine arts terms, this phase is like an artist's laying in the broad outlines of the painting, so that later on she can add color, detail, and nuances. Without a coherent framework grounded in system design principles and fine arts principles, the later stages will tend to be much more chaotic and much more ad hoc. Building this necessary framework prepares the visual management team and the organization for the discipline they will need later on.

Keep in mind that a visual management project may involve one unit of a dozen or so people or may involve a large organization of hundreds or thousands of people spread out over several floors or multiple buildings. Such a project may take a number of years to fully complete. An organization may not know what level of resources it can commit to the project over its lifetime. Priorities will probably change over the life of the project for a variety of reasons that cannot

Figure 5-6. At the MSRB, the lobby display reminds employees and visitors that the board's mission is to protect investors and the public interest.
(Courtesy of Leo A. Daly, Inc.)

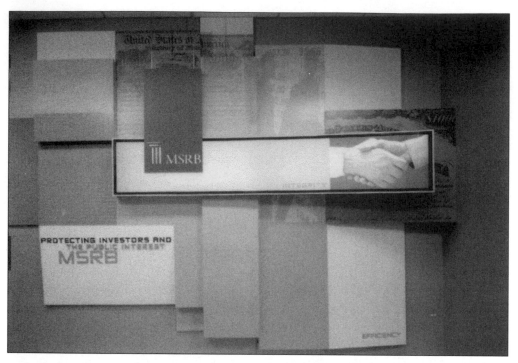

Figure 5-7. The displays and murals throughout MSRB's lobby use computer monitors, plasma screens, LED lights, neon lights, and light boxes to enhance the displays and relate the board's history of carrying out this mission. (Courtesy of Leo A. Daly, Inc.)

necessarily be predicted in advance. Therefore, a solid framework must be developed that will enable the organization to overcome these potential obstacles and achieve the original vision facilitated by visual management.

As phase 2 comes to a close, this framework has been carefully established. The organization has been prepared for change through education and action planning. The physical audit has been completed, and an action plan has been developed. A consistent color scheme has been identified, lighting has been reviewed, and attention has been paid to ergonomic needs. Changes in these areas are under way. The organization has also gotten rid of clutter and established a few key visual themes for future development. At the end of phase 2, employees begin to see some changes, and their enthusiasm typically begins to build. In essence, the groundwork has been laid for real change. Some beautification has probably occurred, but the full impact of visual management on performance is yet to be felt. Chapter 6 deals with the action phases of the real change process of visual management.

Road Map to Visual Management— Implementation

Over the course of the entire visual management development process, a structural system that ensures the ability to achieve the results you want is created or enhanced. Particular attention is paid to the physical plant itself and to the availability of appropriate space for visual displays. As you move forward, you will continually assess the visual cues and determine whether you are connecting the employees to the mission and to the customers. You will also continue to periodically assess whether you have created an environment that celebrates employees, customers, and other stakeholders in ways that enhance your ability to sustain excellent performance. Yet, now that you have a framework, a color scheme, and important data from your physical audit upon which to build your visual systems, it is time to take action to make management visual.

Let's start by looking back at the process road map in Figure 5-4. As we saw in Chapter 5, the initial phases of visual management primarily involve planning and assessment activities: building the team, developing the mission, and creating a solid foundation from which to create a true visual management organization, moving through the bottom half of the road map. Now it is time to move into the upper half of that road map: inspection and alignment, customer and employee focus, fine tuning, and renewal activities. In phase 3 you make the first dramatic visual changes in the workplace, in terms of both physical space and visual themes. In phase 4, you focus on the customer and the history of the organization, and you begin to build the culture of information sharing and analysis that will influence performance. Phase 5 is a fine-tuning stage in which the details are added, reinforcing the messages developed in earlier phases. Finally, phase 6 is a renewal phase: The visual management system is reviewed, revised, and renewed to keep it vital in a changing workplace. These four phases are the focus of this chapter.

Phase 3: Creating the Space

In this phase, an in-depth analysis of the physical layout in which the work is being carried out and of the work-flow patterns is conducted, along with an assessment of the management systems being utilized to accomplish the work. The primary analytic goal is to determine whether the physical space and work-flow patterns are consistent with the work that needs to be done. For example, each team or work group typically has primary responsibility for a particular set of tasks, and it is important that these tasks be physically grouped together so that the team can own the results of the tasks and be accountable for them. Each work group needs a distinct home in which to accomplish its tasks; this provides a clear space that allows the members of the group to concentrate on the job and to engage in the necessary work-related conversations. This distinct space also helps keep people focused on the work and discourages the wandering around and socializing that often accompany a less careful layout.

Reviewing Work Flow and Space

Floor plans must also be analyzed to ensure that the essential adjacencies are in place. In too many workplaces, teams that are interdependent are located too far apart to make the interdependencies function well. Co-location of groups that work closely together or that are serially linked in a core process saves the time and energy required to move back and forth for joint tasks and makes the process smoother. In addition, try to make sure that employees sit near windows in natural light whenever possible, and strategically place file cabinets and shelves between groups to serve as natural barriers.

Office space, too, is assessed in the work-flow audit, in order to determine who needs an office and who doesn't. It is important to ensure that supervisors and coaches have areas of privacy that they can use when they need to counsel employees one on one. If the work itself requires face-to-face meetings or frequent telephone discussion in a noisy manufacturing area, soundproofed offices will make that work easier and the outcome more effective. It is also important to make sure that there are meeting areas for work groups in or near their workspaces so that members don't have to waste time wandering over several floors trying to find meeting space.

As this work-flow scan is conducted, the height of partitions and how they are set up must be assessed to ensure that they are not blocking efficient and effective work performance. High partitions behind which people cannot be seen inhibit a culture of teamwork, but they can be useful for separating teams that are not interdependent or for creating natural buffers between departments. In terms of physical flow and design, the workplace should be one in which people can easily be seen so that they can interact with and talk to other team members. It should be a place in which people are not hidden, so that they can be accessible when they are needed by others, and it should be a place in which managers, when doing their walkthroughs, can easily see how the work is going, how people are doing, where the work is, and how things are fitting together. As you can see in Figure 6-1, QTC has done a nice job of keeping a clear line of sight in its work areas.

In phase 2, the physical audit, the furnishings of the facility were assessed for color and coordination. In phase 3, a further audit of furnishings focuses on whether pieces such as the furniture, the cabinets, and the shelves are functional and whether their condition is consistent with the organization design. An additional brief assess-

Figure 6-1. At QTC, low partitions separate work teams and provide some physical privacy, yet they allow team members to share information easily when necessary.

ment of the color scheme is performed to ensure its consistency. In many organizations, the color scheme becomes uncoordinated over time because people add their own pieces to the visuals. These added pieces tend to be disconnected in color or design, and may not fit well with what has been planned.

From an action standpoint, this is the stage in which actual commitment to the new color scheme takes root. Spray paint is a terrific way to ensure color scheme coordination, and some employees love to get involved in this when work rules and union contracts allow it. Actually changing or renewing colors produces an enormous improvement in terms of supporting the work design and is another clear symbol that things are changing. When the work flows are smoothed and aligned so that people can see and feel the internal consistency, and when the physical appearance and layout support these flows, the consistency brought about by visual management will have a positive impact on performance.

Reviewing Decision-Making and Information Systems

Ongoing assessment of the decision-making and information systems continues in phase 3, with an emphasis on how to use visuals to inform employees and keep them focused on metrics. A review must elicit responses to questions such as these:

❑ What are the best places in the facility to post the metrics? Have these places been used? Are there dedicated areas for group or team results? Can these be created?

❑ Can the metrics be posted in a variety of different ways so that they appeal to as many learning styles as possible?

❑ How do employees know how the organization is doing, both from a team perspective and from a broader perspective?

❑ Do the employees know what the metrics mean and how these metrics can affect them? If not, how will they learn this?

❑ Do the employees know what the goals of the organization are? Do they understand the context of these goals?

Once this information has been gathered, it is time to establish a plan for posting the metrics that includes the type of information to post, the best places to post it, the types of visuals to use, and the frequency of posting. For individual and team results, a posting position within that individual's or team's workspace is critical; for the metrics to have any effect on their performance, teams and individuals must see their own performance results and have them updated frequently. For units or departments, members must be able to see the results and determine how their performance contributes to the overall outcomes. For supervision and management, a greater amount of information is required; this should be posted in areas near them or immediately accessible to them. Not only is it important to begin planning for data posting in this phase, but it is also useful to begin posting some results as soon as possible so that employees become accustomed to seeing results around them. This is the point at which the initial war room concepts are developed. Also, keep in mind that employees who do not understand the metrics must be trained to do so and to know their relative importance, and some attention must be paid to this now.

Reviewing People Systems

Phase 3 is also the phase in which the foundation for the performance elements of visual management is laid. Once the metrics are understood and a plan for posting results has been developed, it is time to look once again at people systems in the organization. The focus of this assessment is on how well these systems for performance management are functioning:

❑ Do people know what is expected of them and how they are doing on both an absolute and a relative basis?

❑ Are employees held accountable for their work and performance, and do they recognize their accountability? Do some employees get lost, and are others able to hide?

❑ Is this a strong, growing, committed workforce, or are there problem employees who are pulling others down?

❑ Is performance being proactively managed?

Great organizations make their expectations explicit and ensure that all employees know what is being asked of them. These organizations clarify their goals and values and the expected ways of achieving them. When people are not working up to expectation, managers in great organizations take action. They deal with problem employees early; they quickly identify who the difficult employees are, and they try to help these employees improve so that their low performance will not significantly affect the morale or the performance of others.

Too often, organizations have created good people management systems, but they simply do not use them effectively. In a visual management environment, as in any good organization, dealing with poor performance and problem employees is a must.

Fit Between Components

As the planning of the details of visual management continues, it is important to make sure that the physical plant and the management systems fit together well. People cannot be held accountable for things that they cannot control. They should not be held accountable for performance issues that arise because of a poorly planned physical layout, physical process, or workspace unless they have the power to change these elements. If a production system is operating at capacity, it is unreasonable to ask for more production without a change in the system. Management systems send particular messages to employees about expectations and reinforce certain behaviors, so it is imperative that these systems be aligned so that people can do what they are being asked to do.

Later, when further details are added to the customer focus, metrics, and employee focus elements, these details must make sense within the overall scheme of visual management. For example, continuous learning is a goal that is common to many visual management organizations, and it is important to guarantee that the physical plant supports this learning goal. Questions such as these help determine the degree of support for learning that exists in an organization:

❑ Where are learning resources located? Is there an office, a division, or a team resource library? Are computers available, and is there Internet access?

❑ Are learning maps, job aids, flowcharts, and other tools readily available to the employees?

❑ Are the materials that foster learning only in writing, or are they also visual? Are they conveniently located where the work gets done, or are they inconveniently located, thus discouraging people from finding the right answer?

❑ When errors are made, do people know about them? Is there a location where people can learn about the most common errors and see appropriate corrections for these errors?

❑ Is a skills matrix maintained that tracks the requisite skills for each job and the skill level of each employee? Is this matrix visual?

As these questions are answered and attention is focused on support for a learning environment, an organization is better able to ensure a match between its overall goals and its management systems.

Keep in mind that at this point in the implementation process, the foundation on which the more detailed and sexy elements of visual management will rest has been built. A framework now exists in terms of light and color: Color and lighting schemes, including the colors of walls, floors, and ceilings, have been selected and provide a base on which other details can be seamlessly added. If, at this point, the organization had a series of walls with different, disconnected, or dark colors or poor lighting, it would be difficult to add effective visual images and cues because the color and lighting schemes would detract from their power. Color and light are mechanisms to connect all of the space and keep people focused cohesively on a single vision.

This base framework is also strengthened by proper space management. As we have discussed, defining important space adjacencies is necessary in order to plan an effective work flow. Before adding new visual cues, be sure you have created good spaces for employees so that they can best do their work.

Congruence and Alignment

Throughout the visual management development process, the implementation team must remember that the primary purpose of combining visual management with good design of organizational systems is to influence the behaviors, feelings, and attributes of the organization's employees so that they will deliver the outcomes that the organization desires. In organizations that are structured properly for the tasks they choose to accomplish, and in which systems are properly aligned, the visuals become the third critical dimensional support and help keep the organization moving forward toward its mission. If the systems, the structure, and the visuals are not carefully aligned, they could be working against one another.

For example, if an organization's mission and vision dictate a tightly controlled environment in which employees follow orders and rules and have little discretion, this would require a particular approach to systems and visual design. If the organization's mission and vision were consistent with an empowered workforce with lots of autonomy and authority, this would dictate a different design approach. The important point is to identify this pattern in advance and then align the structure, systems, and visual scheme before moving too deeply into phase 4.

Any assessment of an organization must always include some attention to this alignment process and its impact on the work and the people. Visitors to organizations can typically sense how systems are working and whether they are aligned well. This does not happen through some great sixth sense or extrasensory perception; instead, it is the result of observations about the people and the place:

❑ Do employees greet visitors cheerfully, or do they merely look down and silently ignore them?

❑ Do the employees have a sense of urgency about their work? Are they attentive to the customers or visitors or their colleagues, or are they engaged in nonwork activities or conversations?

❑ Do they appear to be working hard? Are they focused on the work?

❑ Do they appear to have a sense of pride in the organization, in the mission, in their customers, and in their fellow employees, and do they display this visually as well as in their manner and behavior?

Informal assessment of the people at work will yield a great deal of information about how well the organizational systems have been aligned, and can point out some areas for attention as the visual management process moves forward.

By the end of phase 3, the organization and the visual management team should be well prepared to move forward with the visual plan. At this point, there is a management team that is dedicated to implementing the organization's mission, vision, and core values through visual management. The organization is prepared for change and understands how the planned changes will affect it. Some visual elements have already been installed, and a broad framework has been developed that will support the visual enhancements that are still to come. A plan for maintaining alignment of the organization's management systems with its mission, vision, and goals has also been developed. Space has been carved out for the posting of organization-wide visual displays, team-level information displays, and individual performance feedback. A solid foundation has been laid for the final development and installation of the actual visual images and cues.

Phase 4: Focusing on Customers and Data—Now They Can Really See It

Phase 4 of the visual management process focuses attention on the mission and on the data. This is one of the most robust and exciting phases of visual management, the one in which the majority of the visual cues are added and people begin to see that something is very different in the organization. The initial emphasis in phase 4 is typically on the mission as it relates to customers and other stakeholders, and images depicting customers and their work are installed throughout the facility. Work is also begun on displays tracing the history of the products or services provided by the organization and their link to customers and suppliers. This helps to emphasize both the historical importance of these products or services and their future significance. A great deal of attention is also paid in this phase to developing the data systems that will inform all organization members about performance and results.

Customers, Suppliers, and the Mission

We begin phase 4 with an emphasis on the mission as it relates to external constituents because there are so many employees in so many organizations who do not really understand either customers or suppliers, and who do not recognize the vital importance of such external stakeholders to the organization. Visual management, therefore, is used to raise the employees' level of awareness and focus their attention on identifying and meeting their suppliers' and customers' needs. This helps the employees focus clearly on the linkage between external stakeholders and the organization's mission.

In our experience, we have found that although employees can generally name their organization's largest or most important customers, they often don't know what these customers really expect or how the organization can best meet those expectations. Employees often know more about suppliers than they do about customers, since the products or services of suppliers appear to have more direct impact on their work. Hence, it is important to make sure that employees not only know who the customers are, but know why they are important. Then the organization must decide what customer information to include in the visual displays and what specific messages it wants to send to employees about customers.

With respect to the customers, it is typical to start the visual cueing with the walls, where pictures are mounted that show the organization's products or services and its history. This links the organization and its products or services to its customers in an indirect way and gives employees a sense of their organizational heritage. In manufacturing, for example, a display that shows how a particular product was manufactured decades, or even centuries, before gives people a clear sense of continuity and ties them to the organization's history. In a service industry, tracking how service has differed over periods of time links people to advances in technology or service provision in a positive manner. In the medical field, displays that highlight different ways in which medicine was delivered over time is linked directly to what people do and, again, helps ground their experiences today in the history of the organization. The lobby displays in the Teamsters' headquarters emphasize this concept and reflect their contributions to industry, their vision, and their activism. Figures 6-2(a) and 6-2(b) are examples of their powerful lobby displays.

Once the history has been represented visually, it is time to introduce the customer directly into the mix. In some organizations, the customers are individuals who can be identified and named; in others, they are departments or other organizations. Yet all can be displayed in some coherent fashion that reinforces the message of customer importance. In one company, for example, a display shows a map of the United States with the company's manufacturing and distribution centers carefully marked by miniature corporate logos attached to the map. Customers and suppliers are also identified on the map with photos of their facilities, and links have been drawn to the manufacturing or distribution center with which each is most closely allied for business purposes. This map is displayed prominently for all employees to see, to emphasize for them the interdependent nature of customer and supplier relations. Other organizations celebrate customers in other ways. Amgen's IT department, for example, displays pictures and stories of customers who were helped by the company's pharmaceutical products.

As the basic focus on mission evolves, more complex displays are added. Three-dimensional images, for example, provide an opportunity to place mannequins in real-life settings that reflect the themes selected for the visual displays. Large artifacts such as an antiquated machine or a large, outdated computer capture people's attention and focus it on the roots of the organization or on customers' uses of its products or services. The Silver Legacy Hotel in Reno, Nevada, for example, features a huge antiquated silver-mining machine in its casino, an impressive and evocative reminder of its past. Customers' or suppliers' artwork, displays that highlight the end uses of the company's product or service by its customers, and many other types of displays can be used to reinforce the theme of customers' importance to the mission of the organization. The idea is to try to transform

Figure 6-2(a). Four panels celebrating the history of the Teamsters dominate a wall of the lobby in their Alexandria, Virginia, headquarters. (Courtesy of Leo A. Daly, Inc.)

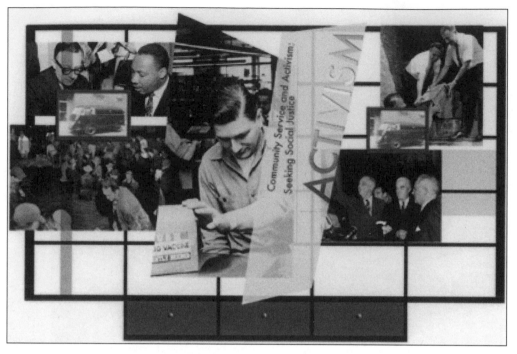

Figure 6-2(b). Each panel commemorates milestones in the Teamsters' development and reminds both members and visitors of the Teamsters' contributions to American industry. (Courtesy of Leo A. Daly, Inc.)

the organization into a clearly focused tribute to its mission, so that employees are reminded of the mission every day, are proud of it, and feel that they are part of something that is important and bigger than themselves.

Once the first displays go up, everyone begins to notice. If the organization has been prepared well for visual management, then employees know what this means and what is to come. Yet employees' reactions vary. Some employees become intrigued with what they are seeing, while others wonder if these are token displays and still others, depending on their prior experiences with change, wonder if management is truly interested in a different approach. No matter what the reaction, the first set of displays is sure to get everyone's attention. It is extremely important at this stage not to merely hang pictures on the wall, for such an approach is of limited value. Only when the pictures and displays are part of an overall theme will they make organizational sense and unleash their true potential. Pictures are pretty and can relieve the boredom of bare walls; themed visual displays that are tied directly to the mission help keep employees' attention focused on the needs and goals of the organization.

Think of this in another way. When museums and galleries display works of art, they do not display them in a random, scattered fashion. There is a distinct context and theme in their arrangement. The works may be organized by style, by time period, by geography, or by artist. While a viewer might enjoy each work of art as an independent piece, the context that is provided by the organizing theme gives the viewer important information about the show. Visual management uses this same thematic approach to provide a context for the visual cues, and that context is what keeps people focused on the issues that are important for the organization.

When the displays start to go up, people react very quickly. After they get over the initial shock of seeing exciting visuals in *their* organization and begin to look more closely, it is not unusual to find that some want to donate their own artifacts or artifacts from their families to the public displays. Of course, these need to be relevant, but most can be made to fit into the design you have selected. All of a sudden, you will move from actively soliciting pictures and memorabilia to display to managing unsolicited donations from employees, customers, and other constituents.

As the visual displays emerge, people's excitement builds, and they begin to offer their heretofore hidden talents to support the visual management effort. Employees with expertise in graphic or fine arts, construction, computers, history, or writing will begin to come forward and ask to contribute. In essence, the base of talent and support for visual management starts to expand beyond the original planning team to the very heart of the organization. This, in turn, enables the initiative to move forward more quickly, as there will be more resources pushing it forward. Moreover, an organizationwide level of enthusiasm emerges that will continue to increase as long as people see that the effort is serious and that management is committed to visual management for the long term. In addition to the employees' becoming involved, it is possible that people from outside the organization will be struck by how unusual this approach is and may seek to donate their time, artifacts, or other resources.

Now people begin to see the real possibilities of visual management. The first three phases of the process are really the building blocks; this fourth phase is when people begin to feel and taste the organization's commitment to this revolutionary approach to managing its environment. In fact, as these displays begin to take shape in the initial target areas, the rest of the organization, which does not yet have displays, begins to look worse. With each new visual installation, anticipation of and pressure for ongoing visual management efforts increase.

As the process continues to unfold, the options for visuals are almost limitless. Pictures, cutouts, posters, paintings, artifacts, display cabinets, dioramas, statues, kiosks, and other means for displaying information visually should all be considered. Kiosks at the Teamsters' headquarters, as seen in Figure 6-3, capture attention because they are different and interesting. In addition, the organization should not limit itself to thinking merely in terms of wall space. Ceilings and floors provide great opportunities to enhance the message. Think of how department stores use banners and photographs that hang from the ceiling to advertise their products. Visit sports arenas and see how they use flags to add color and energy to their events. Burbank Airport, in California, was very creative in its use of an enormous banner to celebrate the centennial of flight, as can be seen in Figure 6-4.

Data Systems and Displays

Although a customer focus is needed to continually remind employees of the customers' importance to the mission, the addition of data systems is even more important for performance improvement. In most organizations, performance data are usually available, but often

Figure 6-3. Information kiosks can provide interesting three-dimensional visual display space. This one, at the Teamsters' headquarters, celebrates the 100th anniversary of the Teamsters. (Courtesy of Leo A. Daly, Inc.)

Figure 6-4. Creative use of flags and banners can draw attention to important information and events. Burbank Airport seized the opportunity to celebrate the centennial of flight and its own 73rd anniversary in 2003.

in a format that is not easy to understand and use. Too often, the data are stuck inside a computer or printed on reams of paper that only a few smart people have access to or can even understand. To reap the full benefit of visual management, the organization must focus its efforts on performance.

One way in which visual management creates this focus is through the development of war rooms, in the tradition of NASA or the Pentagon, in which unit, division, and organization data are frequently, clearly, and consistently posted. War rooms are developed and maintained for three primary purposes in a visual management environment. First, they provide a mechanism that enhances information sharing throughout the organization; once war rooms are established, people know where to find any performance data that they need. Second, they provide an opportunity to teach employees about the big-picture organizational results and their role in achieving these results. This lays a foundation for managing performance and results. Third, they help the organization begin to build a culture of analysis and action, a concept in which all employees are encouraged to act as managers in the sense that they fully understand their role in the organization, they know how their role affects the metrics, and they can easily see what they can do to influence those metrics.

Visual displays are created that build out the data throughout the organization, starting at the broadest levels and then working down to the unit level. The degree of detail and the absolute amount of data will vary depending on the intended purpose. The most complete set of data will be found in the war rooms, where upper and middle managers will gather to see current and historical trend data on performance, review progress toward goals, and plan for the future based on what the data show. Data displays for teams will be more focused in their content and less complex than the displays in the war rooms. Individual performance data will be even more targeted and focused.

Bulletin boards are always a good bet for displaying information that is not immediately time sensitive. Putting together charts and graphs and posting them on bulletin boards can involve a lot of time and labor, so this method of display may be best suited for weekly or monthly updates. Chart pads and grease boards often work well for daily updates, since they can be changed very quickly. UVDI, for example, uses grease boards to track daily production, as seen in Figure 6-5, as well as to capture problem-solving efforts. A different approach would be to use television monitors or other types of computer-based information displays that are updated electronically on a real-time basis.

Data must be carefully displayed on bulletin boards, chart pads, or grease boards to ensure that the displays are uncluttered, understandable, and effective. Those in charge of creating and displaying charts and graphs should have a sound understanding of the most effective way to utilize the variety of line graphs, bar graphs, pie

Figure 6-5. At UVDI, employees maintain production and quality records for their own work areas by keeping a running tally on a grease board designated exclusively for this purpose.

charts, and tables available for data reporting. They should also know what is appropriate and adequate without overloading those who must use the data. Furthermore, they should learn to group the charts by common categories so that how they relate to one another is easy to see. If these displays are then color coded to relate them to the organization's goals and objectives, they can be extremely effective while adding a little extra visual shine to the organization.

Celebrating Victories

Finally, in this phase, organizations need to begin to celebrate the victories that flow as a result of visual management. As noted in Chapter 5, visual management organizations often post "before" photographs, taken prior to the change, next to photos of the current state to highlight the contrast and emphasize the progress they have made. Some develop videos that intersperse views of the physical plant before with current views, again to emphasize the changes that have been made and how different the place is with visual management. These videos are often sent to key stakeholders to announce that this is a dynamic and successful organization that embraces innovation and creativity.

Such celebratory activities help publicize the changes both inside and outside the organization, and the effort to celebrate employees as well as customers begins consciously as the transition from phase 4 to phase 5 is made. As employees' efforts are celebrated in concert with other visual management activities, a domino effect begins to develop.

By the end of this fourth phase of visual management implementation, the organization is changing rapidly. Management systems are beginning to align properly to enhance the organization's mission and vision, the physical plant now reflects the mission and the customers, and people are becoming much more focused on what they need to do to achieve the organization's goals. The data systems are becoming more visual, and the employees are becoming more aware of the metrics. The organization is now starting to see some victories and is starting to celebrate them in a variety of ways.

Phase 5: Focusing on Employees and Fine-Tuning the Details

As the organization moves into phase 5, it really begins to focus attention on the employees and the people systems, while at the same time fine-tuning the visual management elements that were implemented in the first four phases. At this time, critical data have been posted at the team level. This is conceptually very different from the display in the war room, which shows the organizational and departmental data. For teams, the selected data must be directly relevant to what the team is doing. Posted team data typically consist of only a few key pieces of information that are updated as frequently as possible. As a result, people are not overwhelmed, feel connected to the data, and understand on at least a daily basis how their work on the front line affects results.

Measuring Performance

Keep in mind, however, that simply posting the data is not enough. In addition to understanding what the metrics mean, employees must realize that the data are only as good as the accuracy with which they were input to the system. If they are aware of this, then there may be fewer input problems or people may catch them sooner. Employees must also learn and understand the management systems and their relations to the metrics so that they can best utilize the data that are now available to them.

Many visual management organizations conduct team meetings only in locations that have data and information displays, such as bulletin boards, chart pads, and monitors. This is a good way to help employees learn about and become more comfortable with the information so that they will not find it intimidating. As teams spend more time analyzing the data in the displays, they will develop the habit of checking the displays frequently and will build a deeper understanding of all the linkages between the organization's mission and goals, the data, and performance outcomes.

Once the data have been developed and posted, the next step is to link the performance metrics to rewards and recognition in order to ensure that people are truly paying attention. There is a great deal of discussion about the impact of rewards and recognition on performance in organizations, and it is commonly accepted that, for many people, the more tightly linked these elements are, the better the performance. In visual management organizations, it is recommended that this link be established as clearly as possible. In some organizations, this may mean a direct relationship between pay and performance; in others, it may mean a greater emphasis on recognition systems. Whatever can be done to link rewards and recognition directly to the desired performance will support the results orientation of visual management.

Once the reward and recognition processes are in place and functioning well, it is imperative that the results be posted and updated frequently. Some offices of the VA have used the balanced scorecard to track performance and reward their employees. Figure 6-6 shows a team-level scorecard that is posted on a television monitor and updated daily. Team members know in advance that if they achieve their targets, they will receive shares that can be converted into dollars at the end of each year, based on the level of funding available. As you can see, this type of posting can be simple and straightforward, although it is important to do it regularly. People truly become more connected to the organization and take a greater interest in it than ever before, and they work harder to try to achieve the goals.

Phase 5 is the time to begin posting individual performance data as well as organizational metrics. Some organizations actually post this information by employee name, although most do it with a code or within a team or department without attribution. Whatever method is selected, people need to know how they are doing relative to both their performance standards and their peers. Those who are performing well need to know that the organization is keeping a record of their good work, and those whose performance is under par can see where they fit also. It has been our experience that posting individual

	GOAL 9/30/00	Possible Rewards	SCORE	Money Earned
Dept	81.7	$90	94.5	$90
Unit	82	$70	83	$70
				☺☺
		Total $	→→→→→	$160

Figure 6-6. This scorecard is posted on a television monitor and updated daily. It tells team members (the unit) exactly what they have achieved to date in their incentive plan, and how that fits with department incentives.

results helps raise the performance of the bottom third of the workforce and helps top employees recognize that management is serious about high performance. It also sends a message that management sees and is willing to deal with the low performers. Also, because the data are available for all to see, publishing individual performance data helps ensure fair and equitable treatment for everyone.

Because of the emphasis on individual performance, and because the organization is now holding people accountable for their performance, there is an obvious obligation to train people well in how to do their jobs. Development of a training matrix that tracks the skills required for every job and the current skills possessed by all employees is an important part of an overall training strategy. This matrix should be enlarged and posted in a conspicuous place so that management and employees can continually track the training gaps and develop a strategy for bridging those gaps. Development of such a matrix also sends a clear message that the organization is committed to building the skills that employees need in order to perform well.

Once it is committed to training, the visual management organization must make sure that its training methods are appropriate. Too often, training relies solely on the distribution of written training material. The success of this type of training is often uncertain because people learn in so many different ways. Different people use different sides of the brain, and what works well for one individual will not necessarily work well for the next. To further complicate this issue, it is clear that today's workforce responds to different stimuli from previous generations of workers. Remember that younger employees are much more visual than their predecessors; they were brought up on television, music videos, and point-and-click computers. Training methods and materials must take these differences into account.

One approach to training that does so and is gaining in popularity is the use of learning maps. These maps take complex written material and convert them into simple drawings that allow viewers to quickly grasp the key points of a subject. As can be seen in the Learning Map® chart created by Root Learning Inc. of Maumee, Illinois, that is shown in Figure 6-7, these training tools are pleasing to the eye and easy to follow. Employees often hang their learning maps on the wall for quick and frequent reference, unlike written training material, which tends to be hidden away in a file cabinet. Moreover, these learning maps are exactly what newer employees expect and like, given the spirit and culture of the times.

Recognizing Employees

At this stage we begin to focus even more on employee recognition. For example, the development of visual elements such as walls of fame, employee-of-the-month displays, and display cases containing employee awards usually work well to make employees feel celebrated and valued. Columbus Regional Hospital does an exemplary job of celebrating its employees and recognizing them for their contributions. Figure 6-8 provides examples of how the hospital does this in a very special manner.

To expand on the concept of recognizing employees' efforts, some organizations create a room dedicated solely to the employees.

Figure 6-7. The dramatic market changes taking place in the soft drink industry are captured in this Learning Map chart created for use by Pepsi. It captures a forty-year historical time span on one page with sufficient detail to inform users of the key events shaping the industry. (Courtesy of Root Learning, Inc., of Maumee, IL.)

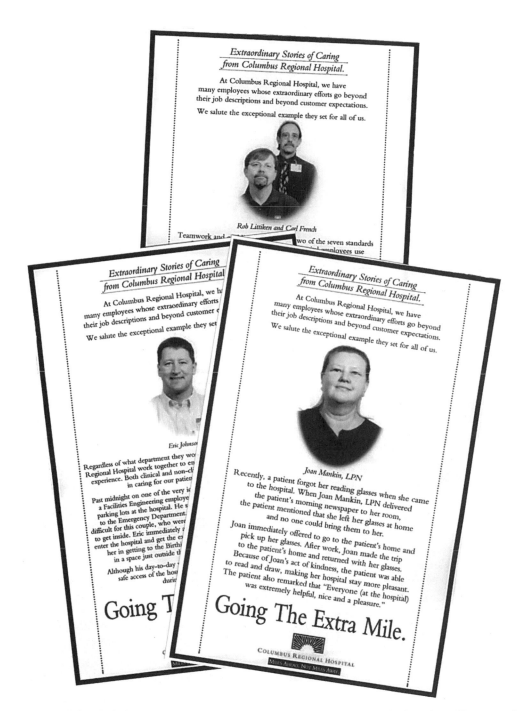

Figure 6-8. Celebrating employees becomes personal at Columbus Regional Hospital, where good deeds and going the extra mile are recognized in print. These messages are posted prominently throughout the facility.

This is typically a room where the employees meet frequently as a group. Displays in this room may include photos of work teams or groups, management, new employees, union representatives and leaders, the children of employees, office activities, and even nonwork events. A particularly memorable display is one that shows pictures from ten, twenty, or even thirty years ago and then contrasts them with pictures of today. The striking change in the culture of the workplace that is shown by such a display is enlightening. As with other visual displays in the organization, variety is important for displays in employee spaces. Organizations should consider using displays that are not limited to squares and rectangles; for example, they could try collages or large cutouts of employees, as shown in Figure 6-9, for

Figure 6-9. It was a heart-warming scene when this young woman, an employee of the U.S. Department of Veterans Affairs, posed with the life-size cutout of her father at the department.

variety. The more creative and atypical the displays, the better they will be received.

Although the creation of a centralized location for employee recognition is important in the visual management environment, employee recognition should not be limited to this one location. A better approach is to scatter different forms of employee recognition throughout the workplace, so that it is clear to everyone that employees are recognized everywhere. There are many ways in which employees can be recognized for their good work, and organizations should be creative about using them.

In one organization, supervisors were given self-stick decals pre-printed with the word *attaboy*. They were encouraged to pat employees on the back with decal in hand to acknowledge work well done, leaving the sticker as a visible reminder for other employees to see. Another organization, whose operations included a small silver-smelting process, purchased newly minted silver dollars for supervisors to award as recognition for services above and beyond the expected in that department. Another created visual thank-you cards imprinted with images that were representative of the organization's mission and gave them to employees, who could then issue cards to each other in recognition of work well done or to acknowledge helpful activities. In all instances, employees found ways to display these symbols of recognition and were proud of receiving them.

An interesting side effect of all of this attention to employees is that as the office decor improves, more and more employees seem to be more concerned with appearances in general, and often seem to dress better. This finding makes the fifth phase of visual management implementation an appropriate time to evaluate the dress code in the organization. Often, when little attention has been paid to the physical surroundings in which people work, a casual and even too informal way of dressing may have developed. In some cases, this manner of dress may even present a safety hazard. If a particular manner of dress is important for the appearance, the safety, or the work of the organization, then, as the physical plant improves, management will be in a much better position to either implement a dress code or change the existing one because of the marked improvement in the environment. Employees tend to be more accepting of dress code changes as the physical plant improves.

Fine-Tuning the Displays

The other major activity in phase 5 involves the fine-tuning of the visual display system. This is the time to review and reassess those elements that were created in the first four phases to ensure that they still fit together well. Are they working as intended? Are they achieving the desired effects? How can the visual elements be taken to the next level?

One of the first things to do when fine-tuning the overall scheme is to start looking beyond the visual and consider how to have an impact on the other senses. Displays become even more effective when they appeal to more than a single sense. Think about how people naturally gravitate toward hands-on displays in museums or aquariums, for example. Adding tactile appeal to a display will capture attention quickly.

Try adding sound and touch to a visual display for even more impact. Do you recall seeing those coin-operated toy horses and vehicles that are often placed outside grocery stores? Once they are fed a few coins, they move and shake and make a few sounds. They are invariably big hits with children and parents because they appeal to several senses simultaneously. With visual management, it is possible to capture this childlike excitement in a variety of displays, particularly if life-size artifacts are included. It is relatively straightforward to take an old machine, an earlier model of a vehicle or aircraft, or some other artifact with moving parts and add a few touches to it to create an interactive display that reinforces the mission and provides people with enjoyment at the same time. The VA's life-size exhibit of a Huey helicopter, shown in Figure 6-10, for example, includes headphones that re-create the sound of the blades rotating for those who climb into the cockpit.

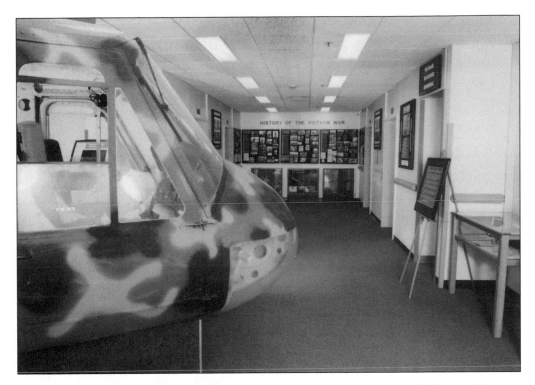

Figure 6-10. The Vietnam War display at the VA includes a full-size Huey helicopter cockpit to which sound has been added so visitors and employees can see, feel, and hear what this helicopter was like for service personnel. (Photograph by Jason Gray.)

Combining the senses of sight, sound, and touch in a single display adds tremendous depth and meaning to what might have already been a wonderful visual exhibit. Think of the addition of sound as an opportunity to inform, to strike a chord, or to get additional buy-in. Add the voices of customers to some of the displays. Give employees the opportunity to hear what their customers have to say, rather than simply looking at them. That is always more powerful. Also consider adding music to some strategic locations. Music is a wonderful way to connect with people.

At some point, typically during phase 5, word about the organization's visual approach to work will begin to spread externally, and it is likely that many outsiders will want to visit the facility. As the word spreads, external stakeholders and other interested parties will focus their attention on the organization and its improving reputation for innovation. As external stakeholders visit the facility, management and employees will have an opportunity to see the effect of the transformation through the eyes of people who have not been close to the redesign effort. This provides a powerful opportunity to learn and make adjustments where necessary.

That being said, it may be even more important to give tours to employees than it is to give tours to outsiders. While employees spend a significant amount of time in the organization's facilities each day, they typically spend most of their time in one area of the physical plant. Employees tend to be keenly aware of the displays in their own area or location, but many of them are only vaguely aware of all the displays throughout the organization. In order for employees to truly see the big picture, understand the full effect of visual management, and grasp how all of the pieces fit together, a periodic tour of the workplace is recommended for all employees.

By the end of phase 5, the organization's transformation through visual management is nearly complete. The management systems are now operating in alignment, the physical plant now reflects the mission and customer at a level that is rarely seen, and the displays appeal to all of the senses. Data systems are consistent and complete, and the employees understand and work to improve the metrics. Finally, the people systems have been refined, resulting in improved attitudes, skills, and performance management; and the employees' behaviors, feelings, and attributes have been influenced to the point where the organization is achieving the outcomes it desires. Yet, there is another critical step to visual management.

Phase 6: Renewing the Process

No change process is complete without some focus on renewal, and renewal is especially important in a visual management environment. This is the time to look back and determine whether the organization accomplished what it set out to do in phase 1 of the visual management implementation. The metrics should tell much of the story about success, and the employees will tell the rest.

The renewal phase provides a time to make adjustments to the system. The organization is now a different place from what it was when the visual management system was initially implemented. Early elements may no longer fit, and new elements may need to be added. At some point, people may become indifferent to the displays; and it continues to be important to find ways to keep things fresh and original and changing.

During the renewal phase, the visual management implementation team must engage in a series of important tasks. The team first needs to assess what the impact of visual management has been on the organization, the units or departments, the work groups, and the people. The team needs to ascertain whether the system is working the way it is intended to work, to determine what is working well and what is not working well. Employees' reactions to the process and outcomes, as well as those of other stakeholders, must be assessed. There is also a need to understand the perspective of the outside world and of those visitors who have seen the facility, since these are relatively unbiased opinions. Most important, perhaps, is the need to determine how visual management has affected performance, in terms of customer satisfaction and other critical metrics. In addition, this is a good time to assess employee satisfaction with the work and the organization.

It is also important to assess other changes since the initial phases of visual management. Often, organizations are facing technological changes, changes in the political environment that affect them, changes in resource levels, changes in leadership, or changes in priorities. Visual management must adapt to such changes in order to stay current and continue to bring meaning into the workplace. An analysis of these issues will dictate the next set of moves in a visual management organization.

You should also pay attention to any signs of complacency among employees. If people begin ignoring certain displays or tuning out others, it is time to refresh the content and presentation in order to retain the fresh impact of visual cues. It may be time to add more detailed information about performance results. Changes in processes or systems may force realignment. Older displays may have become unacceptable given current expectations and expertise in visual management. Technological advances may provide opportunities for new forms of display. The options are limited only by creativity and budget. Yet, action is important in this phase to signal that visual management is an ongoing way of life rather than a completed project.

The renewal phase is also the time to revitalize the visual management implementation team. A number of organizations renew themselves by taking their management teams away from the work site for a few days to plan the future. In these conferences, the organization often brings in one or more outsiders to give the management team a sense of what is going on around it and how other organizations are dealing with performance issues, visual management, and the like. Also, by now, some team members may be tired and wish to back off from full participation in the visual management team, and other people in the organization may have become converts and want to participate more fully. Getting new members onto the team helps ensure that it stays fresh and is open to new ideas. This is also a good time to review the visual management process from another perspective. The team may wish to visit other visual management sites to see what they are doing that could be adapted for its own site. In addition, the team may want to bring in outsiders with expertise in visual management to provide an assessment from a different point of view.

Renewal may also be a time to review and revise the road map. As visual management is fully incorporated into the strategic planning process and becomes part of the annual planning cycle, it is important to ensure that its goals and activities remain aligned with those of the organization. Keep in mind that a road map is typically developed for a particular period of time and set of circumstances, and is usually a good guide for at least three to five years. Major revisions before this time may imply that the visual management process is viewed as a flavor of the month rather than a way of life. Lack of revision after this time may imply that there was an end to visual management, which is also not the correct message. A revised and renewed road map picks up where the original left off and helps guide the organization forward from the success it has already achieved.

From its initial introduction into an organization through the final steps of the renewal phase, visual management creates a process that captures the mission, vision, and culture of an organization and makes it real to the people associated with that organization. Once established, it becomes a true way of life that enhances the organization's ability to clearly identify and work toward its vision and its goals. The reality is that a good visual management process never ends. It is a constant journey toward excellence.

CHAPTER 7

Reality Check: The Nuts and Bolts of Making Visual Management Happen

Every paradigm, every design method, and every management technique must be assessed in terms of its relevance, its applicability, and its fit with a potential adopting organization. This chapter is designed to help you perform that assessment. First, we want you to determine whether visual management is right for you and your organization and whether it will address the issues you wish to resolve. Second, we want you to look at whether your organization is capable of implementing visual management in its current state, or whether it will need to engage in some form of prework before implementing visual management.

Keep in mind that visual management, at its most basic, takes good, solid management practice and uses fine and creative arts to enhance that practice. It is not a substitute for good leadership, for top-notch employees, or for clearly defined goals and aligned systems. The greatest benefit of visual management will be reaped when it is used with competent leadership and strong management systems that support employees' striving to improve their performance. With an appropriate level of commitment, all organizations can achieve the benefits of visual management. Yet we want you to think carefully about whether visual management is really right for you, because it requires an ongoing commitment to ensure its continued success.

Therefore, in this chapter, we pose the key issues that must be addressed before an organization should commit to visual management, and we make recommendations about when and how to adopt the system and when not to. Overall, this chapter will help you assess your readiness, identify key resources that are critical to the success of visual management, and better understand the commitment you are making in adopting visual management as a way of life in your organization.

■ Visual Management Is Not a Department

As you begin to think about adopting visual management, it's important for you to think about the commitments of time and people that will be necessary in order to make it happen. Often, we hear about change processes that people feel have drained time and energy away from accomplishing the business of the organization. Managers report that people have been pulled from their primary jobs to join a team whose sole mission is to manage a new change program. Development of such teams is frequently perceived as robbing the organization of critical staff at the expense of performance improvements. It also appears to add a layer of infrastructure to the system.

In visual management, we identify and build a team to spearhead the effort. But visual management and the visual management team are not a stand-alone system or a department, nor do they add infrastructure. Instead, visual management is a system that supports and is integrated with every other management system in an organization, and the visual management team continues the direct work of the organization. This is the primary reason that other management systems must be aligned before an organization engages in a full-scale visual management endeavor. This is also the reason that people are drawn from across the entire organization to participate in visual management: Everyone in the organization is affected by the changes brought about by visual management, and almost everyone will be involved in some way with its outcomes.

There are generally no employees who are devoted full-time to visual management, however. Instead, visual management uses the talents of employees from virtually all parts of the operation on a collateral basis. People tend to volunteer to support the visual management effort; most of these volunteers have some talents that support the concept, and they believe in the ability of visual management to improve the organization. The size and composition of this group of volunteers change over time. The group tends to grow or shrink in size depending on the tasks at hand, the availability of people, and the phase of visual management in which the organization is engaged. Its composition changes with the rise and fall of interest on the part of participants and with the specific talent demands of the current phase.

Because visual management is not a stand-alone department, it does not have its own set of performance measures. On the contrary, the performance metrics used to determine how successful visual management is are the same measures that the organization uses to track its performance. Therefore, and precisely because visual management works to improve individual, unit, and organizational performance, it is these specific performance measures that will reflect the success of visual management. This does not mean, however, that you cannot tell how well visual management is doing in your organization. Process measures help you gauge the progress of the implementation: You should measure progress against the plan during implementation, sometimes changing the plan and sometimes changing your work pattern to fit your desired outcomes. But the most important measures that tell you that the implementation is working are those that show the increased learning of the employees, the improved relationships with and feedback from customers and suppliers, and the actual performance improvements on critical performance metrics.

Despite the fact that there is no stand-alone department of visual management, there is a group of people in the organization that is charged with responsibility for the process. The visual management team is the linchpin of the project, and this team leads and oversees all phases of the endeavor. Even for the team members, though, visual management is not a full-time job. We estimate that team members will spend no more than 5 to 10 percent of their total work time directly on visual management, although the active time commitment varies with the implementation phase. In fact, no one in the organization is expected to commit more than 5 to 10 percent of his total work time to visual management. Once the system and the associated visuals have been developed, they become part of the work, and updating them helps keep people focused on the goals and on their performance relative to those goals. This updating is not about *doing visual management*; it is about doing the work of the organization.

■ Visual Management Is a Lot of Work

At first glance, a visual management implementation may appear to be simple and straightforward, yet it is simple in much the same way that a great work of art is simple. Great art looks simple, especially to the untrained eye, because the image is so clear, so compelling, and so concise. It may even appear to have been created in a single great burst of energy, though nothing could be further from the truth. Extraordinary skill takes years of training to hone. Great art typically takes detailed planning and, in many cases, frequent midcourse adjustments. If you examine the works of a great artist like Rembrandt, you will discover that he often changed his original design, in some cases over a period of years. Steven Spielberg changed the ending of *Close Encounters of the Third Kind* years after it was originally distributed because he was not satisfied with the finished product. The achievement of great art, great filmmaking, or great music is hard, hard work. So is visual management.

A visual management organization requires an enormous amount of planning. The natural tendency of outsiders who visit a visual management organization is to go back to their organizations and hang up a few pictures, banners, and posters in the hope that this will capture the magic of the place they just visited. But good visual management simply does not happen this way. Visual management is individually designed for each organization based on the mission, vision, values, desired culture, physical plant, and management systems of that organization. Transformation into a real and functional visual management organization requires following the process we have shared with you. While there is a lot of flexibility in the implementation process, that process is what guides the deep and lasting improvements that visual management can bring to the organization. Ignoring the requirement for detailed planning and analysis in favor of hanging a few pictures on the walls will not allow the organization to arrive at the deep cultural changes envisioned by visual management.

To truly implement a sound visual management process, an organization should be prepared for a multiyear investment of time and other resources. Just as an organizational redesign may take years to become fully embedded in an organization, visual management becomes stronger over time. In its own way, it requires as much work as any major change in an organization, in part because it is a more multidimensional approach. Keep in mind, though, that although it is a lot of work, visual management does not require taking large groups of people offline for months or years while it is being planned and implemented.

One of the major reasons that visual management takes so much work is that it is truly a holistic approach to management. All management systems must be reviewed individually and in relation to one another before the actual visual plan can be implemented. Visual management also requires a high degree of coordination between the management systems and different parts of the organization, and it requires continuous evaluation to make sure it is progressing as planned.

■ Commitment Is Critical

As with any other major change or improvement project in an organization, top management's commitment to visual management is necessary for its success. Competing priorities, changes in direction, budgetary constraints, employee turnover, and internal and external skepticism can all result in the endeavor's losing steam and falling by the wayside unless there is consistent ongoing support from leaders at all levels. Top managers set the stage for the acceptance and internalization of any new programs and processes in organizations, and they need to be completely on board with a visual management implementation to ensure its success.

Resistance to change is a fact of organizational life. For every person who is excited and energized by the thought of change and improvement, there is another who has dug in her heels and will not even acknowledge the need for something different. The range of responses to visual management is wide: Some people fight to get on board as soon as they hear about it; some publicly question the entire concept; and others denounce it as the latest fad or as a waste of personnel, time, and resources. Strong, forceful, and ongoing support from upper management will ensure that the program has a solid foundation and will continue to move forward.

This top-level support must be manifested in a number of ways. First, the program must be carefully explained to all stakeholders, internal and external. These stakeholders, and particularly the employees, who will be most directly affected by visual management, must be given time to ask questions, assimilate the answers, and fully understand the benefits of the program. Second, members of the visual management team must be allowed adequate time to accomplish their mission. Visual management is rarely an overnight success, and team members need time to move up a new learning curve and bring the organization with them. Some results will be seen quickly, but the most profound performance improvements will not emerge until the system is well grounded in the organization, and this takes time.

Therefore, it must be understood that patience is required while the visual management team is laying the groundwork and kicking off the process. Third, upper management must be prepared to constantly champion the early victories of the process: The more wins and benefits that can be shown to organization stakeholders, the better the system will be accepted as an ongoing part of how the business is managed. Finally, upper management must make the necessary resource commitments to the visual management process, and this means that it, too, must remember that visual management is not a quick fix for organizational ills, and that it will require some level of financial investment.

■ Visual Management Is Not a Quick Fix

Visual management, at its simplest, is designed to improve organizational performance by rallying employees around the mission and the performance metrics. The tasks involved in implementing visual management take time and are intended to generate long-term cultural change and performance improvement in the organization. Although we sometimes see quick gains from the initial impact of visual management, such immediate improvements are not the intended final outcome of the process; too often, these types of improvements fade quickly if the organization's underlying problems have not been addressed. The careful planning, analysis, and design processes first address the alignment of management systems and then deal with changing the organization's culture. Without this dual emphasis and a long-term commitment, the visual management system will not reach its full potential. And this takes time.

On the other hand, there are some short-term results that we look for in a visual management process. As we work on the process of aligning management systems, we often find some low-hanging fruit—some problems that are relatively quick and easy to address. For example, in several organizations, we found that a public commitment to improving performance at the individual and unit levels brought poor performers forward to discuss their performance problems and try to resolve them. In others, we found that managers and supervisors were making decisions with old data, and we worked quickly to improve the timeliness of reporting to them. We have also found that when organizations begin to post information in a clear and logical manner, this practice often pays immediate dividends. In one company that had been working hard on reducing scrap and waste, for example, we found that workers did not know the cost of the material that was being scrapped on each shift. We quickly helped team leaders create signs to post on scrap bins that simply reported the cost of the scrap material contained in each of the bins. Almost immediately, we saw workers trying to salvage materials that they might previously have tossed into those bins. The level of scrap material began to drop dramatically, and the amount of good final product increased quickly. Workers told us that they had not realized how much money was being wasted until the first signs were posted.

Finally, we also know that hanging pictures, posters, and banners that celebrate the mission, the customers, and the employees will help to build some early excitement that can affect performance in positive ways. As long as the pictures are truly representative of the people and the organization, and as long as they don't highlight an elite few at the expense of others, people begin to feel a sense of being valued and to look forward to the next steps in this transformation process. Finding a few quick wins is a good thing, as this increases the visibility of the process. Yet, for visual management to fully succeed, the organization must remain committed to both the concept and the process for the long haul. Otherwise, if the pieces are not all properly developed and aligned, visual management may eventually lose both its power and its momentum.

■ Visual Management Does Not Come Free

No transition process in any organization comes without a financial investment at some level. Some programs are small enough, or affect a small enough segment of the organization, that they can be funded through existing budget commitments. Others require some significant capital investment and must be approved as special projects. Naturally, because there are so many variables to consider in the planning and implementation of visual management, and because visual management is a custom-designed process, the same cost cannot be assigned to every visual management endeavor. The degree of financial commitment required depends on a number of factors related to the breadth and scope of the proposed program and to the specific characteristics of the organization itself. Basically, the cost to implement a visual management system varies according to the size and type of organization considering the implementation, the condition of the physical workplace or workplaces, the degree of alignment of management systems that is already in place, the availability of visual management skills within and outside the organization, and the degree to which the organization is willing or able to commit funds. Of course, knowledge of the mission, vision, and guiding principles throughout the organization will also have an impact. Let's look at the relationship between these factors and the potential needed investment in the project.

Size and Type of Organization

The size of an organization has an obvious impact on the cost of implementing any new process. The number of people, business units, and locations and the complexity of the physical space will all affect the required investment. Clearly, an organization with 10,000 employees in multiple locations will require a much larger investment than an organization with less than 100 employees in one location. Yet, the investment will probably not be 100 times greater in the larger organization.

In a large organization, we strongly recommend starting with a very limited number of locations, perhaps only one, in order to stay focused and to build credibility for the concept throughout the overall organization. Most organizations should expect to purchase a variety of displays; some pictures, posters, banners, bulletin boards, or easels will be needed in the early phases of visual management. In many cases, organizations already have some of these, and they are often already posted on the walls. Usually, however, these displays are disconnected: They have typically been mounted only to make the workplace look pleasant, without much regard for their fit with an overall design scheme or for coordination among display elements. The degree to which we can retain the picture frames, bulletin boards, or other display media, while replacing the pictures, charts, and other graphics if necessary, will influence the cost of this particular element. In single-site, smaller organizations, the costs for these types of displays will probably average $2,000 to $5,000. In a site with an unusually large amount of space, we might estimate as much as $10,000 for these displays. Some organizations, of course, will spend quite a bit more, depending on the number of displays desired and the type of display media they choose. An organization that wishes to install state-of-the-art video technology or to create an intranet system from scratch, for example, may spend hundreds of thousands of dollars to retrofit an existing facility. Keep in mind, however, that this type of investment is typically made because it will pay for itself in terms of the cost savings it can generate over the long run.

Another factor to consider in determining the required investment is the source of funds for such a project, and this may vary with the type of organization. In our experience, there are a number of sources for funds that may not come immediately to mind in private-sector organizations. For example, grants and private donations have helped fund visual management efforts in a variety of types of organizations. Organizations in the public sector may not feel that they can invest as much in such projects as can profitable organizations in the private sector. However, they may enjoy one advantage over their counterparts in the private sector: They are often in a better position to raise funds from their public sponsors for specific purposes. It has been our experience that once visual management begins and stakeholders start to take notice, people want to donate funds to support the visual management concept. One regional office of the Department of Veterans Affairs received over $200,000 in unsolicited donations toward its effort, for example, once visitors began to see the changes that visual management had made.

Other organizations, too, have discovered outside funding sources that have helped pave their path toward visual management. We foresee the same thing happening at a public medical center, a school, or many other public organizations. In the private sector, we find retirees, local citizens, and other concerned stakeholders who want to participate by donating photographs, artifacts, and artwork to support and enhance the process. So, despite our cautions that a financial commitment is required for the implementation of visual management, keep in mind that the source of the full investment may not have to be the organization's operating budget or a plea for a new capital budget commitment.

Condition of the Physical Plant

It goes without saying that the actual physical condition of the workplace will have an impact on the required funding for this effort. This variable depends primarily on the colors, lighting, carpets, furniture, and clutter of the physical plant. If the physical plant is in good shape with little apparent clutter; the space is well lit; the furniture is professional and functional; and the colors are bright, cheerful, well integrated, and supportive of future visual management displays, little investment may be needed. On the other hand, if any of these design elements needs improvement, the organization may have to invest in improving the space in order to build the requisite framework for future displays.

Furniture and filing cabinets can be painted if they are serviceable and in good repair, but they may need to be replaced if they are not functional or professional enough to fit the visual plan. Lighting is always a major concern in reviewing the physical space. Too often, workplaces are underlit. This detracts from workers' ability to perform at their best and detracts from the desired cohesiveness of the space and its functionality. Lighting investments may be as small as replacing bulbs that have burned out, or as large as replacing lighting across an entire factory floor. In one instance, the investment was as simple as switching on the circuit breakers that had been turned off decades before in an effort to conserve energy. Lighting is always a good investment, though, and it can usually be funded from a building maintenance budget. Color choices, too, are important to the overall visual management scheme. In a space in which there are too many colors or in which there are too many styles of furnishings, color can be used to energize and synchronize. It can be used to tie random components together into a coherent scheme with a far lower investment than the purchase of new furniture or equipment.

The financial investments required for improvement of the condition of the physical space are difficult to generalize. We know from experience, however, that there is lots of leeway in determining how much an organization wishes to spend in this arena, and most cost requirements can easily be met. Costs can range from a few hundred dollars for paint and the rearrangement of furniture and work flow to many thousands of dollars for replacements.

Understanding of Mission, Vision, and Guiding Principles

Many organizations have already gone through the process of developing a mission statement, creating a vision, and establishing a set of guiding principles that are consistent with that mission before undertaking visual management. Some have also invested time and energy in both explaining and selling the mission, vision, and guiding principles to employees, customers, and other stakeholders, so that there is a clear understanding of these precepts throughout the organization. If that is the case, no significant investment of time or money is needed for this process. However, if this has not been done, it is strongly recommended that it be achieved before the organization embarks on a visual management program. The development of such a statement can be accomplished with the help of either an internal or an external consultant and may take days or weeks, depending upon the process chosen and the number of people to be involved in that process.

Because visual management is so intimately linked with the mission, vision, and guiding principles of the organization, this step in the process is critical to its success. We base the entire visual management system on the mission, and we ensure that the goals and performance metrics are aligned with that mission and vision. An organization that does not have a clear concept of its mission, a vision for people to follow, and a set of principles to guide behavior cannot successfully implement visual management. Therefore, this investment is required before the implementation process is initiated. We advocate participative processes for the development of mission and vision statements; the higher the degree of employee participation, the less amount of time will be required to communicate the final concepts. Using external consultative help, an organization could invest anywhere from $5,000 to $100,000 in this activity, depending upon the starting point.

Availability of Visual Management Skills

As visual management unfolds, virtually every organization will discover talent it never knew it had. Employees who have skills in drawing, painting, writing, music, history, and other relevant areas will begin to volunteer their services once they recognize that the organization is embarking on a path that embraces the arts. Finding artistic or literary capacity in an organization is rarely a challenge. Finding the necessary leadership skills for the visual management team is somewhat more challenging, though these skills, too, usually exist in the organization. Over time, there will probably be more people who want to participate directly than are absolutely required.

However, especially at the very beginning of the journey, the organization will have to decide whether it needs the skills and services of a consultant. The consultant's job is to build visual management capability in the organization so that it can effectively manage the process into the future. Given both the novelty and the complexity of the concept and the process, a consultant may be helpful in assessing the organization's visual management potential, in getting the organization started on this new path, and in establishing the framework for the visual management process. This includes teaching the leadership and the visual management team all the details of the process, coaching process development and planning, leading training sessions to increase capacity, and performing many of the other services that consultants typically provide in a change process.

Consultants also may help in preparing some of the initial displays, in ensuring that the transformation moves forward with one vision, and by serving as outside advisers during renewal. There are more direct contact hours early in the implementation process than at the end. Clearly, as the project unfolds and the organization begins to embrace and internalize visual management and develop the internal skill base to sustain it, the consultant's role changes and the degree of contact lessens.

In our experience with the development and implementation of visual management, we have found that the amount of consulting support requested by various organizations in their planning and implementation processes varies over a fairly wide range. However, at a minimum, we find that, first, support is typically requested for clarifying or refining the mission, vision, and guiding principles and ensuring that they are aligned with the strategies and goals of the organization. Second, the visual management team and organizational leadership usually require significant help in the creation of an integrated and aligned framework or platform for the visual management process. Third, the initial visuals are critical, since they set the tone for the balance of the program, and consultants are typically called upon for guidance at this step. The development of the war room is also critical to the success of visual management, and consultants with experience in this sort of activity are very helpful in this process: This step requires the translation of strategy and mission into specific critical performance measures that will be posted and updated regularly and that will be used to guide performance on an individual, unit, and organizational level. As this is happening, the visual plans for the implementation site(s) are also being developed, usually with input from the consultants, who are frequently called upon to conduct the physical audits and interview key constituents because of their familiarity with the process and their independence from the organization. Many organizations also rely on consultants to help them measure progress, to review work completed, and to help assess the organization's needs and support the renewal phase.

These activities vary in duration depending on the degree of internal expertise and the organization's desired level of external support. In general, however, a consultant working closely with an organization that has already established its mission, vision, and guiding principles; that has one or two closely linked sites; and that has a moderate level of internal expertise in managing change, in performance management, and in visual skills might spend thirty-five to fifty direct contact days with the organization over a period of twelve months. In an organization that needs help with the mission and vision development phase and that has less internal expertise upon which to rely, the total number of direct contact days might go as high as seventy to eighty over the same time frame. Future locations, of course, would require a significantly lower investment in consulting support. We also find that it is beneficial to organizations to have the consultants return periodically over the next twenty-four months to help keep the process on track and for renewal purposes.

The bottom line on dollar investment, though, is that visual management is flexible enough to accommodate most budgets, and the costs are spread out over a multiyear period. Some organizations have spent less than $50,000 overall on visual management, whereas others have committed more than $300,000 or $400,000 to the effort over two to five years. Keep in mind, though, that much can be accomplished with some pictures, banners, information displays, spray paint, and reorganization of the workplace, and that consultation support can be tailored to meet the needs and budget requirements of the organization. If we have learned nothing else, we have learned that if there is a will to implement visual management, the organization will find a way to make it happen, regardless of the budget. Moreover, in many cases, if the organization begins to build the displays and the process, the funding will come, one way or another.

CHAPTER 8

A Final Word: Remember, It's Not Just About Looking Good—It's About Working Good

It is sometimes difficult to remember that visual management is a system that is designed to improve performance across organizations. It tends to dazzle visitors with the integrated power of its images. However, the lasting impression that most visitors take from visits to a visual management workplace is not those images. Rather, it is an impression of the employees. Visitors are often struck by how open and friendly the employees in a visual management organization are, and by how committed they are to the organization's mission. This happens because visual management is primarily designed to influence the way employees feel and behave, as well as to reinforce a culture of dedication and commitment that will enable the organization to achieve the outcomes it desires.

As we have stressed throughout this book, the primary goal of visual management is performance improvement. The process drives changes in the structure of the organization, the alignment of operating systems, the physical plant, and the actions and activities of the people. These changes are what drives the performance improvements that we see in visual management environments. Of course, most change programs promise structural and performance improvements.

Part of what makes visual management so dramatically different is the aligned physical, structural, and behavioral environment that it creates. Its physical environment is not simply functional; it is coordinated with the mission and is truly designed to make the organization work better. The investment in visual mechanisms to keep performance metrics visible connects employees to the mission in both visual and visceral ways, and they share information to an extent that is new and unusual. The investment in improvements in the physical plant provides employees with a professional and highly functional workplace. Visual displays focus on and celebrate the organization's employees and enhance their sense of importance and belonging. The commitment to visual management changes the physical environment in ways that also help to reshape the outside world's view of the organization. So, the visual enhancements are a direct part of the performance goals of visual management, and looking good is a secondary, though perhaps the most visible, goal of the system.

■ Visual Management Changes Expectations

People who have worked in visual management organizations have learned to view work and workplaces in a different way. They become much more sensitive to all of the design elements, particularly the visual ones. They come to expect high-quality lighting and a professional environment, and they begin to wonder why every organization cannot be like a visual management one. Bare walls are no longer acceptable, nor are nondescript wall coverings. Uncoordinated displays of products, poorly designed performance feedback displays, and an excess of written instructions and performance documentation become frustrating and demotivating. Once people have become exposed to the world of creativity in visual management, it is often hard to return to the world of the mundane.

For managers, visual management becomes part and parcel of the way they manage and operate. They continually try to improve their work areas, both functionally and visually. They become more mission and customer focused than ever before. Even if they do not themselves possess skills in the fine arts, they liberate those direct reports who do possess such skills and encourage them to participate in improving the workplace. These managers expect information to be shared with employees, and they look for new and creative ways to post the metrics. They also want to make sure that rewards are visible and tightly linked to the organization's goals. They eagerly give tours of the organization to outsiders, and they feel a great deal of pride in viewing the organization through the eyes of their visitors. Eventually, visual management as a distinct concept seems to fade because using visual displays in an integrated fashion becomes second nature, and, although surprising to outsiders, it's the way business gets done internally. Visual management has become a way of life.

■ The Ultimate Power of Visual Management

Every organization has its core systems, processes, and strategic goals. The problem is that the vast majority of employees understand only a small part of the process and are rarely able to relate that part to the organization's goals. As a result, decisions made by management sometimes appear to be arbitrary and inconsistent, leading to fear and frustration on the part of the employees. In a visual management organization, management sets up an overall visual system that helps to explain the various processes to the employees and teaches them how all these processes fit together and how they relate to the organization's goals and objectives. Work areas and work flow are clearly labeled, enabling each employee to see the downstream effect of her actions. Individual performance is often posted so that individual employees can see how they are doing relative to both their individual goals and the performance of their peers. Group performance is posted so that each employee can see how his work and that of other members of the group translates into group performance.

As visual management begins to take hold in an organization, cynicism begins to fade away, and employees begin asking more about the organization's mission and goals. Instead of continually criticizing the organization or simply remaining uninvolved, they begin to change their behavior. We have observed them talk with others about the mission, watched them give tours of their facilities, and seen them come forward to bring in personal artifacts, books, and other items in their possession that have organizational meaning and that they want to share with the organization, other employees, and stakeholders who come to visit the organization. We have watched as they begin to open up and share anecdotes about how they were able to help their customers. Visual management affects employees positively; they regain trust in the organization, and they begin to feel part of an active and positive culture. As this happens, it becomes clear that employees are really hooked on the process and are developing a greater sense of pride in their work and in the organization. They want to make a difference, they feel connected, they feel proud, and they are willing to take the extra steps necessary to improve results. And visual management begins to show up on the bottom line.

If an organization has all of these elements working together, all the necessary management systems coupled with all the visual systems, then the organization becomes a work of art itself. The elements become aligned, both visually and organizationally. When that happens, visual management creates a top-performing organization—one that works as good as it looks.

Twenty Questions (and Answers) About Visual Management

Whenever we visit an organization to introduce, make presentations about, or support visual management initiatives, people usually want to spend additional time with us discussing the process and how to make it happen. They usually have quite a number of questions, too! Some questions are quite specific to the particular company or site we are visiting, but some are raised by people who want to learn more about visual management in general. There are about twenty questions to which we are nearly always asked to respond, and we include them here, with our responses, for your information.

1. "What do we do about employees' wishes to personalize their own space, especially when what they want to do doesn't match our chosen visual scheme?"

Employees should be allowed to personalize their own space in some manner, particularly the space that immediately surrounds them. You should, however, ask them to personalize that space within the spirit and scheme of the visual management plan. They should follow the overall color and style schemes as closely as possible. Some organizations even provide small items such as personal tack boards and photo frames that match the new décor for employees to use. The challenge is different depending on the type of personal space an employee has.

In an office environment, for example, customers and many other employees don't even see an employee's personal space; it is often shielded from public view by file cabinets, partitions, or other dividers. In these cases, guidelines about personalization of workspace can be fairly simple. Ask people to keep clutter under control, to maintain a neat work area, to work within the color and style scheme defined by the organization, and to refrain from inserting personal items into the public space. Where the personal space is shared or open to public view, there is a greater challenge. In these cases, more detailed parameters should be established to guide the personalization of workspace. Ask that anything that is posted or displayed be neat, clean, and professional and that it not clash with the overall visual scheme planned for the site, particularly in terms of color and style.

Small bulletin boards consistent with the overall color scheme should be made available near personal workspaces. When there is no designated place to post notes, minutes, reports, and so on, lots of paper is taped or tacked to walls. Like the wire coat hangers from dry cleaning establishments, this paper has a bad habit of multiplying overnight, leaving walls cluttered, disorganized, and not particularly useful. In addition, when tape is removed, the paint often comes with it. This, combined with the puncture marks from overuse of tacks, damages the surfaces and detracts dramatically from the newly created physical environment.

2. *"Our union is extremely resistant to posting individual performance, and it is telling us that we cannot do it. What can we do about this?"*

When you post individual performance results, they are not attributed to individuals; names are not attached to the results, and the intent of performance posting is not punitive. It is critical to understand this. The goal is to manage overall performance in a positive manner, and that cannot be done without seeing the individual performance levels that are combined to give the output. Also, bargaining agreements generally do not specifically prohibit the posting of performance results. However, some organizations have managed to foster an environment of distrust between management and the bargaining unit, and this often will create some stumbling blocks for any change process.

In an environment in which every employee knows how he is doing relative to all other employees, there is a clear focus on understanding and meeting performance expectations. Union leaders should also know that when performance is posted individually, this creates a transparency of results that makes it nearly impossible for anyone in the system to engage in favoritism. All employees, managers included, become more accountable in the visual management system because they have immediate and consistent feedback about how they are doing. Performance issues are dealt with directly, following procedures established by contractual agreement, and in a fair and equitable manner. Typically, when union leaders have been involved early in the visual management planning process, they understand the rationale behind the posting of individual data, and they become more comfortable with the practice.

3. *"I want to implement visual management in my organization, but I don't think I will be able to gain top management's support. What should I do?"*

You should implement visual management within your own sphere of influence. You can do a lot with very little investment. Then tell other people about it, sharing your wins with the process. Over time, people will begin to take notice of the changes you are making and the results you are getting. As the culture in your area begins to change and your performance begins to improve, you will have some clear, measurable results to share. You are more likely to be able to convince top management that this is a viable and appropriate process when you have some hard results to back up your request for support.

4. *"Our landlord is not very flexible about making changes to the physical plant. How can I get the landlord to agree to the upgrades required by visual management?"*

Start with a few simple changes that will gently persuade the landlord that this is in her or his best interest. Get rid of the clutter, brighten the place up, and add a few photos that convey a sense of pride and accomplishment. Help the landlord understand what you are trying to do; share photos of successful visual management organizations, and demonstrate the benefits for the landlord of having a clean, organized, bright, and improved physical plant. Involve the landlord in the visual management planning process early on; make sure she knows what it is that you plan to do and how. And don't plan to spend the landlord's money on your project unless the lease specifically promises this. Do, however, offer to partner with the landlord, and remember to share credit for some of the improvements.

5. *"Our employees think we are diverting funds from purchasing computers and other needed items in order to implement visual management. How do we respond to this concern?"*

In the beginning, the workforce may be skeptical of visual management. Employees may see it as another "flavor-of-the-month" program, particularly if you have adopted and discarded several other change processes in the past. You will have to learn to live with a bit of early skepticism. More important, though, you will need to show people that visual management is the way you will be doing business from now on. They need to see it as an integrated part of operations, not as a separate line item in the budget. Further, if employees in your organization do not understand the basics of organizational budgeting, help them learn about the line items that are important. Help them understand that most organizations set aside funds to improve the physical plant, and that these funds will now be channeled into a program that will directly improve the bottom line.

6. *"Our headquarters has heard that we are implementing visual management and wants to know why we plan to redo our environment. It feels that our space is just as good as that of other locations. How do we respond to this?"*

If headquarters sees visual management as an interior decorating project, then you have not done a very good job of explaining your intent or the process by which you will generate performance improvements. It's time to do more education. Create and deliver a specific, focused, and informative presentation targeted specifically to the headquarters group; use this book to guide you, or call us to help. Be sure that you frame and explain this process in terms of performance: The visuals are a mechanism to focus attention on performance improvement and the achievement of the organization's mission. Explain visual management clearly and explicitly, and provide lots of examples to illustrate that the funds are not being used primarily to improve the physical plant, but rather to improve the organization's performance. As proof, cite some of the organizations highlighted in this book that have successfully used visual management. The bottom line is that you are investing in the bottom line, not in a physical redesign.

7. *"We tried sharing information before and it didn't seem to work. Why should it work under visual management?"*

In all likelihood, information was shared in the past without development or appropriate use of the requisite support systems. Visual management emphasizes sharing information effectively. Information sharing works in this system because it is shared in easily understandable formats (i.e., visually), it is shared in multiple ways to meet the needs of people with different learning styles, it is accompanied by training that explains to people what the information means, and it is clearly linked to performance and rewards so that people see the importance of learning this information. Essentially, visual management teaches people what information they need in order to deliver the expected results; teaches them to locate, understand, and interpret this information; and teaches them how this information is relevant to them and their work. Once people have learned to use the information that is being shared, they come to depend on it. This helps to institutionalize the new information-sharing protocols in the system.

8. "If we aggressively track individual performance as you suggest, won't we wind up firing a bunch of people and destroying morale?"

Good question, but keep in mind what we said earlier: The goal of tracking individual performance is to help people improve their own individual performance in order to boost organizational performance. The intent has never been to have you fire people in whom you have invested heavily, and visual management is not a downsizing program. In many organizations, however, there is a group of people who have never been told that they need to improve their performance. Often managers have not identified what it would take to help these individuals succeed. You need to make sure that you are not one of these managers, and there are tools that can help you improve your ability to track and deal with performance. Keep in mind that by tightly tracking individual performance, you will be able to identify problems early on, and you will be in a better position to assist struggling employees. Remember, the goal is to improve performance, not to terminate people.

In the rare instance in which you have to take action against an employee, other employees will consider your action to be fair and appropriate. Everyone will know that you are tracking performance by the numbers and that you are making a good-faith effort to help all employees who need it. When the rare action to terminate a low-performing employee is taken, the usual reaction from other employees is, "What took you so long?" No one likes being held back by low performers.

9. "With all the demands we are currently facing, how can we possibly find the time to implement visual management?"

Organizations invest thousands and thousands of worker-hours in un-tried and untested approaches to management in a desperate attempt to improve performance. Visual management involves a minimal investment of time and uses tried-and-true management principles and practices. It is an integrated support system for your organization that focuses all efforts on achieving the mission and goals you have set out to achieve. It is not an add-on activity; it is a set of practices that enable you and your employees to work more effectively. The better question might be, "Why wouldn't you find the time for a system that significantly improves your productivity, quality, and customer satisfaction?"

10. "We haven't gone out of our way to hire artists in our company, so how can we deal with the fine arts aspects of visual management?"

You may not have gone out of your way to hire artists in your organization, but we bet that you have an incredible amount of talent, including artistic talent, in your organization that you don't even know about. In many organizations, the demands of the day-to-day work seem to stifle creativity, and employees don't see much point in bringing their talents to the attention of management. But look around your workspaces at what people have brought to work with them. Chances are that you will find lots of creativity there: the cartoon sketched by an employee at a particularly dull meeting, the careful and exuberant use of color when taking notes on the chart made for a team meeting, the hand-embroidered scarf worn around someone's shoulders, the clean lines and careful organization of one department's bulletin board, or the spectacular photograph on an employee's desk. There is truly a lot of talent in your organization. Once employees have heard about visual management, and once they see that you are serious about it, they will bring their talent forward and offer to participate. In the rare instances where such talent is not available, or when you are waiting for it to surface, an appropriate consultant can fill the gap.

11. "If visual management is so great, why haven't more organizations implemented it?"

Visual management is a relatively new concept that is not yet well known. As with any new idea, it takes time before people understand and accept it. As people learn more about visual management, as they see it in action and come to appreciate its results, they grab onto the concepts and want to run with them. We have already seen lots of interest in the process, and we have heard from many companies that they are ready to pilot the process in their sites. We anticipate rapid growth in the next few years.

Also, visual management needs a solid foundation for effective implementation, and this takes time to develop and implement. To date, relatively little has been written about visual management, so organizations have not had a clear road map to help them understand how to implement it. Our goal is to share the power of visual management with organizations in all types of environments and to share the principles and practices behind it in clear and uncomplicated terms so that many more organizations will learn about it and have the opportunity to implement it.

12. *"What happens if the leader of the visual management initiative leaves? Will we be able to maintain the momentum, or will it simply fade away?"*

Strong, supportive leadership is important to the success of visual management. There is no guarantee that the process will survive the departure of the key visionary leader unless the new leader has been fully introduced to the process, is prepared to take over, and is accepted by the organization as the one to continue the effort. This is one reason to select a strong visual management team. That being said, however, as visual management takes hold, many people will climb on board to champion the process. They will want to see it continue, even if the original leader leaves. When a new leader enters the organization, sees that visual management has been successful, and also sees that it has strong support throughout the organization, it is likely that she will continue to lead and support the concept.

13. "This seems so complex, and it functions on so many levels, that it just feels overwhelming. How will I ever be able to pull this off along with all of my other assignments?"

Visual management is not an additional assignment; it is a way of doing business. It is not a stand-alone approach to management; it is an integrated approach. Connecting people to the mission, celebrating employees, sharing information, and holding people accountable will make your life easier, not more difficult.

Visual management is implemented in much the same way as other new initiatives or endeavors. It requires planning, coordination, and support. It is not implemented all at once, as a shock to the system. Rather, it is implemented carefully and systematically to make sure that it does not overwhelm the employees or harm the organization in the short term. It is up to the visual management team to ensure that the necessary steps are accomplished in a logical and integrated fashion, taking into account your workload, staffing, customer demands, and other organizational priorities.

14. "We were really excited after we visited a visual management site, and we immediately wanted to get started on our own project. But when we got back to our offices and looked at all the space in front of us, we froze. Management has agreed, people here are interested, but what do we do now? We just don't seem to know where to start. What do you suggest?"

Getting started is probably the most difficult part of implementing visual management, and it can seem overwhelming at first. You are not alone in those feelings. From an artist's perspective, the most difficult part of painting is staring at a large, white canvas and deciding what to do with it. It's not much different when you consider redesigning an organization, though the canvas is not blank. You just have to take a couple of steps: Identify the team, read everything you can get your hands on about visual management, talk with people who have done it, start to document the physical plant as it exists today, and begin to clear away the clutter.

If you and the visual management team feel that you need help in getting started, then you should consider bringing in a consultant with expertise in visual management. As with any new project, a consultant can help you get started, avoid some pitfalls, frame the issues, and decide on the next steps. If desired, consultants can also assist an organization throughout the most challenging phases of visual management implementation.

15. *"You indicated that visual management could be implemented for less than $50,000. But we have less than $10,000 to spend. What should we do?"*

Start anyway. Many changes can be made for little or no money. Removing clutter, organizing the workspace in a more logical fashion, hanging photos highlighting the mission and the employees, sharing information, and tracking and posting data can be accomplished through a variety of methods and means. In fact, one of the fun parts of visual management can be finding creative ways to improve the organization without additional funding. You might consider partnering with others who share some common ground (e.g., the union or key customers), relying on internal talent, recycling existing displays, or taking advantage of requests for internship opportunities from schools in your area to garner support for the project. As visual management begins to take hold, it is likely that more money will appear, either in the form of outside contributions or from additional internal funding commitments.

16. *"On the one hand, you talk about holding employees accountable, and on the other hand, you talk about celebrating employees. Doesn't that seem contradictory?"*

All good organizations do both, and yours should be no different. To ensure top performance, all employees must pull their weight. You need to identify those individuals who are having problems and find a way to help them improve their performance. If you can't help them improve, then the organization's performance will suffer. Moreover, the rest of the employees will wonder why they are working so hard when others who are unwilling or unable to perform are being paid the same, so that their lesser performance has no consequences.

The vast majority of employees, though, particularly the top performers, must be celebrated. They need to know that the organization appreciates their efforts, that they will be recognized and rewarded for these efforts, and that they will have opportunities for growth and learning. This sends a strong message to everyone that high performance is valued by the organization. If the high performers don't believe that their efforts are valued, they will eventually lose energy and wonder why they are working so hard. Over time, they may decide to leave, and the organization could suffer enormous harm from this draining off of talent.

17. *"Some of our employees think this is a silly and unrealistic approach. They want to know why we are doing all of this artsy stuff when we are fighting for our survival. How should I respond to this?"*

Visual management is about performance, which is the key to any organization's survival. It's artsy only in the sense that it uses fine arts principles to bolster performance. It actually relies upon tried-and-true management principles, then leverages the fine arts to take the organization to another level.

If you look around you, you will find that nearly every discipline is becoming more visual. With society changing at such a rapid pace, people are relying less and less on the written word. Cable television, computers, the Internet, cellular telephones, and PDAs have changed the way we access and receive information. The glut of information that we receive from such media is overwhelming, and we all feel overloaded. We are looking for new ways to make sense of the massive amounts of information that we receive, and the best way is by tapping into the phenomenon of visual literacy. People today have become visual learners, and visual management leverages this learning trend to help focus their attention visually on what is important for organizational success.

18. "I can't even draw a straight line, nor am I particularly creative. I can see where some of the creative types might want to do this, but I'm more a bottom-line type of individual. Why should I want to implement visual management?"

You may not feel overly creative or be able to draw a straight line, but these abilities aren't necessary to succeed with visual management. It is likely, though, that you manage people who have a variety of talents that are not being utilized. Why not use all of their talents in an effort to unleash the untapped capacity and energy within your organization? If you can get employees involved, you can create buy-in and commitment to the process, as well as tap hidden talents for contributions to the plan. People generally want to contribute in new and creative ways.

19. "Visual management makes perfect sense to me, and I'm anxious to get started. I keep singing its praises, but the other key leaders who are my direct reports don't seem to get it. How can I convince them that visual management is the way to go?"

Sometimes people have to hear things from others outside the organization in order to be convinced that a new idea has merit. In all likelihood, they don't understand the concepts as well as you do, nor do they have the same experiences, inclinations, or training as you. Your best bet is to expose them to other organizations that have implemented visual management. Bring in visual management experts as speakers or encourage them to tour a visual management facility. An outside perspective may help them begin to see the power of visual management, to recognize that it does work, and to be far more inclined to support it.

20. *"Okay, I'm convinced. What do I do now?"*

To quote the Good Witch in *The Wizard of Oz,* "It's always best to start at the beginning." Put your visual management team together, have the team members read this book, follow the steps described in Chapters 5 and 6, and have fun. Good luck, and let us know how it is going.

NOTES

■ Chapter 2

1. For an interesting and somewhat controversial discussion of generational cohorts and their differences, see Neil Howe and William Strauss, *Generations: The History of America's Future, 1584 to 2069* (New York: William Morrow, 1991).

2. See Ron Zemke, Claire Raines, and Bob Filpczak, *Generations at Work: Managing the Clash of Veterans, Boomers, Xers, and Nexters in Your Workplace* (New York: AMACOM, 2000), for practical advice on dealing with these differences in the workplace.

3. All data quoted in this section, including those in charts, are from the U.S. Census Bureau, *Statistical Abstract of the United States*, 2002, unless otherwise noted.

4. William H. Whyte, Jr., *The Organization Man* (New York: Doubleday, 1956).

5. U.S. Department of Commerce, National Telecommunications and Information Administration, *A Nation Online: How Americans Are Expanding Their Use of the Internet* (Washington, D.C., February 2002), http://www.ntia.doc.gov/ntiahome/dn/html.

6. Michael Medved, "Television News: Information or Infotainment," *IMPRIMUS*, Hillsdale College, 28, no. 7, July 1999.

7. The Associated Press, "NBC to Air 60-Second Minimovies," *Burlington Free Press*, August 5, 2003.

8. Ellen Galinsky, Stacey S. Kim, and James T. Bond, "Feeling Overworked: When Work Becomes Too Much" (New York: Families and Work Institute, 2001), http://www.familiesandwork.org.

■ Chapter 3

1. For some excellent work on organizational culture, see the classic work of Edgar Schein, *Organizational Culture and Leadership,* 2nd ed. (San Francisco: Jossey Bass, 1992), or a current version of Terrence E. Deal and Allan A. Kennedy, *Corporate Cultures: Rites and Rituals of Corporate Life* (Cambridge, Mass.: Perseus Publishing, 2000).

2. For an overview of the original work in sociotechnical systems theory, see the work of Eric Trist, *The Evolution of Socio-Technical Systems* (Ontario Ministry of Labor, 1991), or Fred Emery, *Characteristics of Socio-Technical Systems* (London: Tavistock Institute, 1959).

3. William O. Lytle has done a careful job of explaining accelerated design processes in several articles and monographs. One of these, titled "Accelerating Organization Design: Choosing the Right Approach," has been published as a chapter in M. M. Beyerlein et al., *The Collaborative Work Systems Fieldbook: Strategies, Tools, and Techniques* (San Francisco: Pfeiffer, 2003). Also published in this text is a useful article about participative design methods by Donald W. de Guerre, "The Participative Design Workshop and Its Variations."

4. Richard H. Axelrod, *Terms of Engagement* (San Francisco: Berrett-Koehler Publishers, 2000).

5. Paul Gustavson is president of Organization, Planning and Design, Inc., in San Jose, California. For a full description of the OSD model, see P. Gustavson, "Designing Effective Work Systems for Greenfield Sites," *Expansion*, November/December 1988, or Paul's Web site, www.organizationdesign.com.

6. See, for example, G. D. Galsworth, *Visual Systems: Harnessing the Power of a Visual Workplace* (New York: AMACOM, 1997).

◼ Chapter 4

1. "War room" is a term that is commonly used in business, government, and education to describe a central location dedicated to performance data and their assessment. We use this descriptor in visual management because of its common use across a variety of industries and companies. However, one might as easily refer to these areas as "performance centers," "performance spaces," or "bunkers," or use any of a host of other names. The point is to have a central and accessible space dedicated to the posting and use of performance data on a regular basis.

2. Source: Company Web site, www.ZiLOG.com.

3. R. M. Felder and L. K. Silverman, "Learning and Teaching Styles in Engineering Education," *Engineering Education*, 78, no. 7, pp. 674–681, April 1988.

4. Susan M. Montgomery, "Addressing Diverse Learning Styles Through the Use of Multimedia," working paper, University of Michigan, 1995; http//fie.engrng.pitt.edu/fie95/3a2/3a22/3a22.htm.

5. J. R. Katzenbach, *Peak Performance* (Cambridge, Mass.: Harvard Business School Press, 2000).

6. C. L. Cole, "Building Loyalty," *Workforce*, August 2000.

7. "Gen X Loyal to Employers That Treat Them Well, Survey Says," *Houston Chronicle,* December 10, 2001, http://www.chron.com/cs/CDA/ssistory.mpl/business/1166757.

◼ Chapter 5

1. "What Does It Mean to Be a Regional Hospital?" Columbus Regional Hospital, 2003.

2. UltraViolet Devices, Inc., http://www.uvdi.com.

3. Environmental scanning is a technique used in large group change processes. It is designed to gather a great deal of information about the internal and external operating environments of the organization in a relatively short time frame.

INDEX